# BRIDGES OF GLASS

## GEORGIA MITSI

*Bridges of Glass*

Published by Lee's Press and Publishing Company
www.LeesPress.net

**Lee's** PRESS | *A Premiere Self-Publishing Services Company*

ISBN-13: 978-1-964234-14-4

*PAPERBACK*

*To my parents who gave me roots.*

*To my children who gave me wings.*

# TABLE OF CONTENTS

CHAPTER 1

# CHASED

*Chased! That's how I always felt. I lived all my life, feeling that time was running out and finally it became a reality. While I was still young, this feeling seemed like a false alarm, but now that I have lived more than half my life, slowly turns into a reality that is hard to ignore. I need to find a solution soon that could reverse the predetermined course of my life. I need to find my inner peace and stop running like a hunted animal mainly from myself, because suddenly I am so exhausted.*

*I remained clueless when my "guardian" died unexpectedly and left me alone with our 10-month-old son. My life changed drastically from one moment to the next. The day after the funeral, I couldn't even open the garage door because there had been a power failure. I didn't know the security code to our safe, how to set up the air conditioner, how to turn on the television system, where he guarded the extra keys, the gardener's phone number, how many bank accounts he had, his lawyer's name. I found myself in a huge house within a tiny little one, completely dependent on myself and soon with many large bills. When the generosity of friends ran out, I realized I had to lead a normal life again and soon moved into a small apartment in a normal neighborhood far away from the hills of my dreams. There were moments when I felt nostalgic for my golden cell, but most of the time I enjoyed full control of my simple life. Time passed, and my son lost his first, second, and third tooth and we celebrated his first, second, third, and fourth birthdays in different houses and different states. And just as I was getting used to my beautiful routine and my difficult role of single mother, I met Theo.*

*I married Theo or Theodore, a smart, sweet, very successful second-generation Greek man who loved to work and who spoke little Greek. I met him by chance when I went to get my tires changed. Another chore that I had never done before. That day, seeing his open smile, I decided to leave behind all the bad parts of my past life and make a conscious effort to live a normal one with a sweet dose of boredom. The time had come for me to try!*

*I am not curious to see how this story will end. I wish I had the opportunity to rewrite it. To write my story from the beginning! Fresh, without memories, vested expectations. Just hoping to have a great time and laugh with my heart. To have fun before I die. Have some fun before I die! Why should only Sheryl Crow have this opportunity? I cannot have 7 children for obvious reasons, but never wanted a $50M villa, I have almost forgotten that I once lived in such luxury, but I spend wonderful moments at my place with its three bedrooms!*

*I had a wonderful childhood, living with my parents in a house of 80 square meters. I had no yard or dog, but I had a lot of love and affection. My elementary school stood and still stands in the shadow of a castle of the Venetian era. In this castle my friends and I made our first strolls as kids. In this castle I had my first kiss and felt like a real princess. I still feel really calm, almost happy, when I'm in my small hometown, perhaps the poorest in all of Greece. When I return to my childhood room, packed with memories, beautiful and ugly, books, records, mementos of a bygone era and life, I still feel it's comforting fragrance in which I was always lost. Inside this room,*

*I dreamt of writing my first book and I did it. Secretly, in an old notebook camouflaged by a Physics book. Within this room, I dreamed of travelling the world and I managed to do it. Within this room, I dreamed of winning an Oscar. This last goal I have not fulfilled. At least, not yet! But I managed to check off many of the goals on my long list.*

*Now everything is awfully relative! Success, age, cold, heat, beauty, pain. For some people you look old already at 18 and they rush to lecture you on the responsibilities that you need to undertake. At 27, 30 at most, these people expect you to be already married and up to 40 to have at least 2 children older than 5. For others again, at 20, even 30, or even 40, you remain not old enough, not mature enough, not quite ready for serious things. Of course, as I said before, everything is relative, because if you're 30 and are compared with your father who is 70, then, clearly, you're not yet old enough. Lately, more and more, I enjoy the company of much older people. Is that another sign of growing older or perhaps a last attempt to feel young again? Or maybe trying to see what is behind the evolution? Of getting prepared for the big changes?*

*Already approaching 45, she has a son of ten years old and a daughter of four and she has been married for five years. This is her second marriage, but her previous life had so much drama that she prefers to forget it. Right away, without any other description or further information, you have before you a mature woman, somewhat chubby, who emits a softener's fragrance even though she employs a Filipino maid. But if the description includes that she is a single woman, over 40, employed, making EUR 500, with a car, even of a small horsepower, and with her own home–such weird situ-*

*ations do occur in Greece—then right away you get an image closer to Cameron Diaz...even though some clear differences appear. Of course, if you place the "softener" next to Cameron Diaz, Diaz is the winner, no question about that, but it always helps if you look like her a little bit. But the balance begins to lean heavily toward Diaz, she whispers Tania Tsanaklidou's song "I grow old, mommy, I am Nice, new but unfortunate ... " and when she is ready to shout, "I grow old, mommy!" She remembers her childhood best friend who at 45 now keeps calling himself a "troubled child" (the status on Facebook? another paranoia of our times). She sends him a message, while enjoying her first cup of coffee in the morning: ""I'd rather be a troubled child than a troubled adult, my dear Chronis!"*

*On top of that, while browsing the Facebook profiles of her old friends, here comes Dimitroula with a swollen belly. What amazing things the Internet, Facebook, technology does! Regardless of how much one hates technology, it amazes everyone with the changes it brings to interpersonal relationships. (In other words, one hates technology, when for instance, the apps are stuck, or when formatting doesn't work, and therefore a man's assistance is needed, especially Théo's. He comes as a savior to solve any problem in 2 seconds, whereas she would have to spend forty plus minutes without even figuring out the problem).*

*Take Dimitroula, for example, a fellow student whom she had not seen for more than ... hmm, many years. Dimitroula discovered her on the Internet world and sent her a friend request. She accepted her request with joy, especially because she had spent many years buried, almost forgotten in her deep hole. They update each other on their lives, avoiding the touchy*

*areas because even 20 years later, the dark past cannot be for-
gotten. So, they tackled the precious and fleeting moments
like what you're doing, where you are, if you're having fun
etc. With great dignity and enough curiosity, they followed
each other's life. So, one day she discovered that her friend was
pregnant. And she is really pleased because Dimitroula's
photo with her proud belly and smile convinces her that she
is happy. But are other details necessary? Why does she need
to know on which month her pregnancy is? It is important for
her to know how many pounds Dimitroula has gained or is
it worth it to mention that she craved ice cream and sent her
husband to search for it in the middle of the night and also
what flavor was it? Do we need her life's 24-hour broadcast-
ing? All this information can only serve in an endless cycle of
gossip, and it's been a long time since she has stopped participating in this feast of gossiping.*

*So, as she was browsing the photographs of all of her Face-
book friends had posted on their walls, she saw their summer
vacation destinations and felt homesick, something rare lately.
She was especially carried away by the photos of one of her
nieces whom she had only seen once when she was born and
then she stumbled again on Dimitroula's photos before her
pregnancy while eating some local delicacies, very much like
insects and she had a smile as big as a football field. The
photo was probably taken before tasting the local dish. Anyway, that's not our business. The point is that while she had
a hard time feeding her baby son, Dimitroula jumped from
tree to tree and ate strange insects ... something that made
Calypso so jealous! Mostly because whereas they both were
the same age, Dimitroula could do every single stupid thing,
but she wouldn't even cry so that her children wouldn't see*

*her cry. Think about it, it's the worst kind of jealousy one can experience, that is, to be jealous of someone not because of his or her bigger house compared to yours or more money or a better car, but because of his or her carelessness. Indeed, you can't buy carelessness with savings or loans at better rates. Either you have it, or you lose it forever!*

*So today, when she saw Dimitroula pregnant, Calypso rejoiced and grieved at the same time, because she had no idea how much this event was going to change her life, the baby's life, and their life. She had no idea how painful it would be for her to start feeling that she would have more in common with her mother than with her younger sister! How right was her mother each time she used to say to her: "The time will come when you'll understand me when you'll become a mom." At these words, silly Calypso would laugh back then, refusing to pay attention to the importance of her mother's prediction. Fortunately, Dimitroula managed to go to Costa Rica with her fiancé. Calypso and her beloved will need to wait until their retirement to go to Costa Rica and unfortunately at 75, jumping from tree to tree is not the best thing to do.*

*Have you noticed that as you grow older the summers no longer have the same smell? They rather don't have any scent at all, they fade… like everything, I vividly remember the scent of the summer afternoons in my small hometown where nothing happened, nothing moved; when all adults slept despite the lack of air conditioning, whereas all children behaved mischievously though silently, or they would simply keep quiet squeezing their hands tightly and devising their plans to execute immediately after the end of the silent hours. When I would not have time to read my novels, which had already kindled my imagination, --no Internet existed at the time—I liked to iron. I spent so many summer afternoons ironing. Aside from helping my mother, I enjoyed the power that ironing gave me. I could create order from absolute chaos. The more flattened the linen was, the better I felt, although I would be drenched in sweat. Sweat, adolescence and lack of deodorant, even with frequent showers, was not an easy thing ...*

*It seems to me that the yellow linen that I so much liked to iron with the special product we had then, saved my parents from many teenage explosions. Unfortunately, the trick doesn't work anymore. Now when I decide to iron, something increasingly rare, I don't experience the feeling that everything is under control anymore. Perhaps I exhausted that feeling at a very young age. Perhaps I've understood that increased entropy and not order is the normal scenario at the end... Or perhaps I may be afraid of accepting my new role as a mature woman, spouse, and mother ... Who knows? But at 25 years abroad I haven't slept on ironed linen, because even if you have help at home, ironing costs money. Amidst all the high monthly bills I pay every month, I refuse to add an extra one for ironing. And we are just fine! We sleep peacefully, make love more and more rarely - but the linen is not to be blamed for this. We play with the children, we work on our i-pads, laptops, i-phones or skype, while we still dream, fight ... just like those who sleep in smooth sheets!*

*Apart from the fact that within 40 days I will have to find a solution in order not to go back to my old job, two things preoccupy me lately. One is that I am growing old. The second is how to adjust to the idea that some things I had dreamed of never happened, which hurts me so much that often tears come to my eyes.*

*I think sometimes about annual eye exams. The technician told me that at some time I would have to also add lenses for presbyopia. He added stoically: "The process occurs over time." I thought that the comment was not for me that he must be referring to the patient next to me, but nobody was sitting next to me. Something similar happened to me, during my last pelvic exam. I said that I was 40 years old, without even thinking about it. I covered everything by saying that it was an important age for me because I had given birth to my daughter. What a year, how would it be possible to forget it? As far as the mammogram, I was told that I had delayed it, but I could do the colonoscopy after... Fortunately, there are still some things for which I can consider myself still young (!) ... mainly medical exams.*

*As a matter of fact, why the hell are they asking you how old you are since they already have your file with your date of birth? Do the math, sweetie, and find out about my date of birth. And if you must be taken for surgery, I understand it. They remind you of your age in any possible way just to prepare you. In other words, before you enter the operation room, you have to realize that you are not a youngster anymore and thus anything can happen. Whereas in Greece no one gives a damn about whether you will end up horizontal after surgery or not, in America you are bombarded with tons of questions and unnecessary paperwork, not because they care about you of course, but because they are afraid that a relative might sue them and then they will have to pay.*

*I write my age on the paper to accept the fact easier, but to no avail. The age of 50 hits me like an avalanche leaving me cold, unlike the number 38 that fits me perfectly. As far as the signs of menopause, I make an effort to ignore them, but my hormones have gone crazy once again. Should I find a lover in my 70s to feel better? I have even forgotten this flirtation game ...*

*The time that passes troubles me more and more because I don't have a specific plan for the future. Besides, I have a pretty long list of things we should have done and probably will not have time for. For a period, I was overcommitted to work and dreamt of becoming CEO and then fell to the phase of absolute disdain and began to believe that I would be happier as a stay-at-home mom. I tried this and after a while I was ready to start eating the walls. Some days I don't fit in my clothes, other days I fly in clouds of happiness, trying to find the right idea to start my own business and every day I wonder how my life would have been if I had never gone to America ... or even if I had decided another time to go! The return is always in the back corner of my mind, but I don't worry as often as before.*

*What scares me most is that we age alone, without family and friends. And time seems harder here in America. No breaks, no October 28 and November 17 and carnival of Patras and Clean Monday. Neither for St. Dimitrios and St. Anne or St. Constantine and Helen, you have to have five celebrations and get 5 gifts; the only birthday parties to which we are now invited are those of our children's friends. And unfortunately, these types of gatherings are not among my favorites. I treat them like antibiotics or rather as stress practice because they make me feel unbearably bored.*

*It is incredibly difficult to make friends, like the ones you had in school, at the University. To be perfectly honest, it's diffi-*

*cult, but not impossible. You need a little luck and a lot of patience. When you do not have to go on holidays, or to birthdays, weddings, baptisms and funerals, the only thing that can get you out of your daily routine is the appointments with the doctor. Which doesn't seem like much of an occasion for celebration. Especially after a certain age, they seem like strange temptations of fate. Oh, and I'm lucky this year! Pap smear or mammogram is negative. The occasion for celebration ... again I outsmarted Death, the sneaky one!*

*You want to celebrate, but with whom? One has a meeting, the other is busy, the other has to go to the child's workout ... You end up rejoicing at life's prolongation. It's of no use, however, since you don't have anyone to share it with. In the long run the only people who are happy are your own children, just because they need you awfully. Studies have shown that people with reduced sociability live less long. I feel that their conclusion is correct, but after thinking about all these moments that I was wounded by friends, I'm not entirely convinced about how much better our life in Greece would be.*

*We all have friends, siblings, and cousins but all comes with a price. Here at least we do not get tortured by foolish things like: "Did you see your cousin Takis? He built a house with a swimming pool, while you, useless one, you've only gotten debts on your credit cards!" Or: "Look at little Katerina, she's got a Chanel suit," or: "George got promoted to Prefect of Central Greece." An endless game of comparisons, like what you did, or they forced you to do when you were little, and you met your classmates after summer vacation. "Did you see how much taller little Helen became?" She gained at least 8 inches..." Without taking into consideration that her parents were two-feet tall and it would be scientifically accurate to argue that little Helen would become taller than you. And now, this small comment was more than enough to destroy the thrill of your summer vacation while you were focusing on your bad luck and not your genes which were responsible for making you gain only 5 inches. Not to mention the brutality of puberty when you returned to school with all of these relentless comparisons of butts and thighs.*

*"Oh my God, have you seen how many pounds Dina has put on? How come, she became like that!"*

*You knew well that when you left them, they would judge you. You knew well that the 3 pounds you had put on would not pass without being noticed and at that moment you were feeling all the ice creams, the grapes, and the watermelons that you had devoured the last 3 months suffocating your throat. And of course, who could forget the books little John was reading every summer! No matter how hard you tried, little John would always receive the prize.*

*Living on the other side of the globe, you rid yourself of all these stupid things that might destroy your day and your mood and minimize the possibilities of disputing with your family and friends. They don't know anything about your life, and you don't know anything about theirs. Everything ceased the day you left. Your age, your psychological maturity and even your shape. For all of them, you remain the twenty-year-old girl, with the fresh young face and the frightened eyes. However of course, everyone sinks into his own world and in the long run this bind fades. Even if you stubbornly struggle to keep it alive, what you end up loving at the end is only a memory. You don't notice many storms and neither they do yours, while sure enough you rid yourself from the extremely boring and loaded with hypocrisy family meetings. You don't attend the show "we are a nice, loving family" for about 24 hours once a year, and moreover and more importantly, you don't participate at all!*

*At times, you feel a panic attack which stings you like a dizzy wasp on your forehead, powerfully enough for you to take notice, but harmless at the same time. You start thinking that your life will suddenly end, and you feel that it is your duty to tell some friends how much an important role they played in your life, how unique moments they managed to offer you mostly despite themselves. Because this is exactly what counts... the mistakes! I remember the first time I visited London, I found myself in a friend's car that was taking us somewhere. It didn't matter where; I don't even remember what street we were on. The only thing I remember was that we were hearing music by Piazzola, we were silent in an empty, big street with wonderful buildings and the entire scene --1-2 minutes long-- was as if it was specially created in order to celebrate my first night in London. Like a climax in a movie, where music expands everywhere, and you remain stunned at the actors' faces which remain overwhelmed with emotion. I always felt the need to tell that friend how unique he made me feel that night! I never did it. I thought I would see him again. When we met again after 15 years, it would have been inappropriate and unbearably romantic to thank him for that night.*

*Like when I learned to fish for sea urchins in a small bay outside of Athens with a friend of mine. Primitive satisfaction, indeed, "I catch my food by myself." What freedom and power! A magic moment, especially for a child who never played in the streets and never climbed any trees. She looked like a lady; I looked like an ugly duckling. It's amazing how you can develop strong bonds with others in such a short time. When all parts fit together, time is of no importance. To that particular friend of mine as well as to some other people who gave me unique moments, I never said thank you, and even in some cases where I did say it, it likely sounded like formality.*

*There are cases where people have the tendency to live situations as if taken from Brazilian sitcoms, Turkish, or Greek soap operas. Lives loaded with pathos and intrigues. Surely, interesting lives as well as distinguishable from the rest, the mortal ones. No matter how she envied that type of life, on the other hand she very well knew that too much drama was not for her tastes. But again, those tearful eyes, the desperate kisses, the wharfs, the airports, the melancholic stations were intensely charming. Her imagination created dramas and passions with the above ingredients, and she wished she could be the protagonist in these scenes.*

*Her wishes came true at the end because she experienced a generous amount of drama in her life. She indeed felt the separation and the abandonment, and her eyes became full of tears and closed doors abruptly and drunk till she dropped and hoped she was not born...but every time there appeared to be a reason for her to continue to live. And when finally, the trains, the airports and the ships did not take much time to be transformed from doors of escape to dream to working places, the magic was gone and suddenly I came to adulthood. I came to it a little bit late... And at some point, the moment also came when even the idea of a flight, even if it were for leisure purposes, was almost despicable to me.*

*I don't know who said and why "Be careful what you wish*

*for," but he was right. It is enraging to spend an entire life trying to reach a point and when you finally attain your goal, if you are lucky, to realize that it was not what you expected. Amidst tons of to-do lists, I should remember to look and find the wise man of this maxim 'We set off for another place and life takes out to another place instead." Before continuing my narrative, it suffices to say that this line sums up my life perfectly. Instead of marrying the rich lawyer with his office in the central square, the villa with the elevator in the suburbs and access to the best boutiques of the area, I emigrated and before attaining a comfortable lifestyle, I was shopping for several years at one of the Dollar Tree stores.*

CHAPTER 2

# MUSIC & LOVE

*I have the feeling that my childhood is filled with sounds. There are no memories in my mind from beloved people and things. Only sounds... music, songs and specific melodies form the path of my life from the subconscious to the first moments of my self-awareness. My mother, as she was coming from a family of musicians must have kept singing to me from my embryonic life. My grandpa, a successful merchant and well-known cantada singer of the time refused during the Occupation years a tenor position in Italy because his mother did not be separated from the youngest of her seven children no matter how she risked losing him forever from the bombs, the massacres and hunger. Thus, my grandpa did not become a famous tenor and I myself lost the unique opportunity to be the granddaughter of the first Greek tenor who reached the Skala of Milan. Instead, he preferred to fill in our house and the streets of my small birthplace with God-sent melodies. Because he hardly ever remembered the lyrics, mainly he was whistling! Every morning he would start his day with a squeezed lemon in a glass of warm water and a melody. He would leave whistling; he worked whistling and was coming back whistling. He made a fortune and three daughters, and he worked hard, without heating, in the small shop that he locked with old-fashioned locking bars when all the next shops had beautiful window displays, for sixty years. He stopped only when a stroke met him deceitfully.*

*Besides then my mother and my grandfather, I also had a grandma who was different. We never made cookies, embroidery, and pillows together. As a strong and tough woman that she was, I remember her telling me fairy tales that scared me almost always. That's why I was avoiding her somehow. My grandma with the fairy tales-thriller I appreciated her many years later and fortunately she was still around when I decided to talk to her. Nevertheless, her influence on the first years of my life was zero. Yet the fact that she alone of the women in her village, instead of staying home to cook, clean and wash the pants of her brothers, she preferred to go with them to the fields riding her horse had created besides admiration also a strong role model that I finally followed much later in my life.*

*At my family environment however there existed also other unique people. I grew up amidst cozy hugs, sweet kisses and songs. The songs that tirelessly my two young aunts were singing to me. It was the new wave period, and the rhythmic ballads were perfect for a newborn. They had not inherited the talent of a melodious voice, but they were singing to me with love, and this is something that even a baby can feel it.*

*Thus, we arrived at my father's. He did not come from a family of musicians, but my grandfather, I was told was the best mason of the area. He was building houses from crafted stone, true masterpieces! But my great grandfather was also a great artist. He was a carpenter. He was so good that he even made and decorated his own coffin because no one else could compete with him in the art of wood and passion. Therefore, my father also was coming from a family of artists with a woolen blanket and a tuxedo, the same for weddings, funerals and graduations, his sole dowry from his student years, had dreams and passion to offer to his first kid the best he could. He was devoting to me endless hours in his effort to awaken me spiritually as soon as he could. But how much Mythology and*

*Classical Music can possibly absorb the mind of a baby? According to my father, his own baby was not a common baby. This is why he used Theodorakis as a lullaby for me. "Sleep in my lap like a star tonight. And he was bringing me up with Elytis, Seferis and Varnalis. And then I lived in a world in which none of this was appreciated. The line "No value remains in the world at all" might explain the strange turn that our life took.*

*As progressive minds they were, my parents, grown up in the echo of the war and tormented by the Junta, were living the new reality with greed and participated in the parody that demolished the country. Both of them along with so many of their generation wanted to change the world. They did it however without any plan and wisdom. They started the demolition starting by the traditional customs. They did not want thus to name me according to the custom that dictates the name of one of the grandparents. Despite the overall disappointment, the decision was made. And the name of hers, Kalupso! To avoid however potential hysterias and other diplomatic episodes—not everyone was ready to embrace all the changes—the name that was heard in front of both the God and the people was Vassiliki-Kalypso. This was not a name, but a monstruosity. A chimeric creature with representatives from the generation of Centaurs. Half man, hald horse. Half terrestrial, half mythic. Half prosaic, half dreamlike. Half real, half fake. As a result, the initial idea of my parents was transformed to a nightmare for me. Half of my relatives called me Vassiliki and the other half Kalypso. The worst, however, is that still up to this moment in my life I have not understood which role of the two is more suitable to me. I tried to walk on the earth the moment the air was lifting me upwards. The result? My life was full of jumps. In between people, countries, feelings. And thus, my mother's initial fear that I look like a leaf that goes with the wind was proved true.*

*One of the winds that influenced my life threw me in his path. It was a Siroko, a southern hot and deceitful wind. When I first saw him, I did not feel the storm that the winds were preparing for us. He was tugged within his melodies, lost in his world, concentrated in his music image that his hands were creating. Sensitive and sweet like a kid. For Kalypso he was a challenge, for Vassiliki a danger. Yet Kalypso, blinded by passion, shut Vassiliki's mouth, opened a ditch deep down in the earth and enclosed her there, trying to ignore her. In vain Vassiliki was trying to react in her dark damped prison. The echo of her voice was piercing Kalypso's terribly weak, yet quite chilly guts.*

*Ignoring the voices, shook powerfully the rich mane, took the shield of the youthful years and since edged the mighty arms of her youth, landed spectacularly in front of him. Hair long, unruly, with golden touches, as if they had trapped pieces from the summer sun, flanked by two slit eyes whose gaze promised a thousand and one nights. Two purple lips as if they were painted with blood, waited to quench their thirst. Skin shiny and bright that only youth can give you. With eyes firmly focused on the trophy, impatient, but mostly stunned by the music, she swore that this man should have been hers. And as it is in the fairy tales, before the second moon was completed, they had already become a couple. In fairy tales, of course, because of the old habits and customs, the coveted mating would happen only when the lad had passed the tests and the twelfth moon would have been completed, but Calypso and Michalis were two young people, full of flame and the sooner the better for the fire to take place.*

*Michalis didn't have a mythical name, nor any mythical prop-erties. When he was strumming his guitar, however, and as he started to compose, it was as if she were diminishing Apollo's beauty. This is at least what she believed. On stage he seemed like a mythical hero and that is where Calypso first saw him. She waited until the end of the concert and after passing through the Rocks of Sympligades-she could have seduced even the worst monsters; she managed to approach him and captivate him. Something about him attracted her to him, something strange, hard to explain. It was so powerful that prevented her from seeing his true dimensions. An out of this world image lit up in her brain. That's love. She was com-pletely indifferent to its real dimensions!*

*"Talk to me. I love it when you talk. I love to listen to you. Tell me about colors, smells, tastes, pleasures. Play their music for me. Create life images for me. Refresh my mind. I want to fly away with you. Only you can do it. You know it and I feel it because I want to love you. I love you with a different love. That will never change. I love you with a spontaneous love like a child, an irrational madness, endless like the sea." I was writing to him. In one of the many tearful letters of those days, when people sent letters they could think and express them-selves with more than 40 characters. And at the end of the relationship, if they were lucky, they would receive a nice par-cel with deposits from their exposed souls. Reading random letters in retrospect, I wondered in the depth of my heart whether my words were exactly what I was feeling or what I would have wished to feel at the time. And then I wondered if as we grow up, we simply changed the way we fall in love or never fall in love the way an inexperienced heart and an*

*even more inexperienced mind do.*

*Regardless of how flattered he felt by her love, he was not in a position to share her ecstasy. He was in a hurry to manage everything, and Kalypso was running to catch up both him and time. He had to make recordings, do interviews, photo shoots, seminars, collaborations, trips whereas she was trying in vain to combine her life with his. In other times, their differences might have been a reason for them to come closer to one another, but for these particular people there were gaps that by no means could be bridged.*

*Kalypso was a girl approaching twenty years old and Michalis around 35. The age difference was not huge. Huge was the difference between their way of thinking and their lifestyle. She was a kid "worthy" of her generation, spoiled, immature, clever and cultured, very sensitive, without plans for the future —since her parents had persuaded her that everything was under control, but mainly without the minutest idea about the world. He, however, was full of concerns... for the rent, the motorcycle installment, his rehearsals, his performance, his career. Kalypso had her eyes pinned on him while he was looking for the next opportunity. She was a Law student and her daddy's office was waiting for her in the central square. Even the potential groom was waiting for her. The son of her daddy's partner. Good boy, a lawyer too.*

*However, she had other plans. Even before the winds of life had brought Michalis to her path. This entire plan seemed to her like a death rehearsal, but she was looking forward to life. To seeing! Things and people would be different. She did not know exactly what she was looking for. She had a clear idea nevertheless what she did not want to do in her life. She wanted to escape from the pre-determined plan. Her heart was in desperate search of love, absolute abandonment, absolute pain. To begin with. Until she matures, at least psychologically speaking. And Michalis appeared at the right time. At the time when all the cells of her body were seeking love. Thus, with the mind being free, her body ready and carried away with a child's enthusiasm, she started her journey with him.*

*A journey different from others. Unique experiences and feelings, but Kalypso was so naive! She didn't know that crazy love may end up disastrous. She couldn't even imagine it! She immersed herself completely in this strange relationship like a kid in front of a perfect cake with none nearby to advise her how much to eat. In the crazy itinerary she was starting, no one was found near her to tell her that sometimes love cannot and shouldn't overcome every problem.*

*"I wish I could go back in time. To be given another chance! We were a lost cause although we had met under fairytale-like conditions. And usually, fairytales have a happy ending. Despite the fact that our first time was indeed my very best first time. Despite the fact that we didn't need to talk to understand each other. Even though we were together, time seemed almost motionless. However, lost cause, my love. I knew it. From the very first morning I woke up next to you. This is why I think I love you even more than before. I knew that I had to fight with time. I could not let him play against me. The more time was running short, the more my love was extending, growing like a sea lost in the deep horizon..."*

*And amidst all this, she also led her own daily typical life that she was struggling to change. She wanted a little bit of color, of light so that she could start little by little to look like him -- multicolored, luminous, and so creative. Her exams and classes maddened her, her friends disturbed her, and her parents brought her back to a reality that didn't suit her and reminded her rather of black comedy. She had no confidence in speaking to and getting advice. All of a sudden, she found herself in a relationship that she wanted badly to maintain, but in which she knew that love alone would not suffice. She could not understand why. She had to discover and activate her mature side, which unfortunately was in sleep mode. The only thing that she managed to do was to present her spoiled, girlish side, which she had polished until then.*

*"If I wanted to keep you, I would not lose control. My role was that of the strong one. I am sorry to acknowledge it, but I wasn't. I told you about this. You didn't listen, you didn't understand. You only told me that I was strong and that I could rely on myself. I knew this, my love. I knew better than you that I could. However, you were afraid of me depending on you. How wrong you were! I was not looking for a foothold, honey. I was looking for a human, to show him my real face. For a friend who I wanted to know me, without my everyday defenses. I wanted you to accept me. I was not longing for a fake "super self," my love.*

*However, I let it go, without fighting. You wanted to be with a super self, so I struggled to create one. That way I learned to feed your hungry imagination with pictures, scenes, and big words. I learned to limit my spontaneity. To control my mood swings and my words. To increase my endurance and tolerance. To adapt comfortably to unprecedented situations. To hide my negative mood well, not to drink wine, to quit smoking, become a vegetarian, love simple restaurants, ask before deciding what to wear, liberate myself when making love. I learned to stand your strange programs, your long absences, your late arrivals to our date, your dislike for Rembetika music taverns, your joviality with the female gender, your tendency to forget me when you had business meetings, your persistence for a clean kitchen once we've finished eating, the constant and intense refusal to read my written concerns.*

*I was willing to adapt to your life because I fell in love with you. And it was a great challenge for me because it was my first time. Back then I was interested in fitting in with others with my own quirks. And I succeeded for the most part.*

*She had never rested on her feet; it simply was not needed. Every fiber of her body was looking for him. She was trapped once again into what she longed to do and to what she was when he had met her. He was not analyzing it so deeply. He liked her the way she was. Even in her own tragedy he found her charming. And above all, he wanted her. The smell of her body, the texture of her hair, the small gap between her front teeth. They looked like they were reading the same novel, and one was constantly ahead of the other. Her efforts to create an image that she thought he'd like did not bring the best results. She was trying too hard and unnecessary.*

*Changes that occur in ourselves, no matter how small they are, are products of processing that happens to every one of us in a unique way, derived from very personal experiences and events and usually they occur over time. First, in order to happen and second, for us to realize them. Calypso kept unconsciously changing, but consciously, she presented a completely different image from who she was meant to become. She didn't realize it, she thought everything was under control. In addition to that, Vasiliki had long ago become muted. Nor did Michael feel the intense struggle that was taking place inside her. He was only seeing a beautiful and sensual creature who behaved mainly like a kid and sometimes like a woman. He sensed that inside, a woman was hiding whom he could love madly, but he didn't know how to extract her or how to stabilize her.*

*I knew it, too much freedom would place a distance between us. We adored freedom so much, perhaps our insecurity was greater. The fear of falling into deep love and starting to behave in a human way, more tenderly, less egotistically, was perhaps the reason for our love to be turned off. We were trembling with fear, thinking that we might cease to be important to each other. And all because we were thinking that some people shrank, and love was to blame. We were forgetting, however, that others, through love, touched perfection. But we were "superior types." We were not a typical couple.*

*We were "deep thinkers." We had our philosophical queries, crazy dreams, difficult questions, all without answers. We were liberated from base emotions, such as jealousy, sneakiness, lies and such. Lying next to each other after a sweeping love, the telephone rings and you talk to another woman who insists on meeting with you at a definite place where you'll be tomorrow, whereas I maintain indifference. I act as if I didn't care, however, the thought that I do not have any power on your heart kills me. I am powerless when it comes to words. I am not ready to listen to any answers. I don't ask who she is, what she wants from you, what relationship she has with you. Absolutely nothing, although my heart suffers from a huge pain that takes my breath away. I turn my back on you, pretending you are a stranger to me, and I bet that when you hang up, you will hug me. And you do. You hug me and kiss me gently on my back and I am assured that the other woman is not simply an acquaintance. I smile because I won the bet and want so badly to cry out of joy and pain together, but Judas' kiss gives a strange pleasure. I dream that I stab her with a knife many times.*

*"I close my eyes and think that love alone can drive me mad! This is at least what I believed until the moment we separated. Then I learned that the pain of loss can undo you for good! The moment came at some time that I lost you and thought that I had lost the entire world. As a matter of fact, the world has always been there and waited for me to teach me little by little that I still had a lot to learn and to endure. I wonder sometimes even today how my life would be if we had managed to stay together. If we had grown old together in a small house with our little grandchildren going around on our feet, asking us over and over to look a million times at the pictures from grandpa's concerts. I wonder how many books I wouldn't have written, how many trips you wouldn't have made! How different our lives would have been! We chose another lifestyle. Deliberately, not deliberately, it doesn't matter anymore. We went through different life situations; we met different people, and we escaped the monotonous everyday life strife. We spent our lives enclosed in rooms, trying to justify the happiness of others, maybe for us too, following crazy, sometimes even inhumane schedules. We contributed to the altar of art!"*

*But one day he was gone. We worked together for ten entire years, and I remember he just did not show up one day. I waited for him at his office to do the last corrections. We were about to finish the editing of his last book. We had such a strong and particular relationship. Beyond the limits of respect, love, awe. I loved him, and I admired him. But most of all, he was the person who made me want even more. To become the utmost of myself.*

*The only person who told me: "Go ahead! I believe in you. Whatever you do, it will be successful. Only don't ever abandon the effort."*

*Truth or falsehood, it did me good. I believed in myself, and I found my lost passion. And we found him later that day with a rope around his neck. He did not seem as if he would depart in that way. That way did not suit him.*

*"No, I did not suspect anything! We lived together, yes... but I was not with him in the morning. I had left earlier. I had to take the kid to the doctors. He had a fever. I am sorry!"*

*He was a joyful, dynamic, creative man. Only something in his dear slightly short-sighted eyes seemed different. He had something more intense than he should have.*

*Still today I wonder whether it would have been up to me to prevent this ending. Whether I could have predicted what happened. For many years such thoughts tormented me. Sometimes at night he still comes to rest upon my eyes like a veil of tears. Maurice had done so many things for me and I was not nearby at the only moment he may have needed me. And supposedly I knew everything about him. About his three failed marriages, the underage girl who, in her attempt to seduce him attempted suicide, his only daughter whom he adored but who was taken from him by her mother, due to a mistake of his youth. About his books, his bright career, his travels, his expertise on things that only connoisseurs know, his love for cold pizza in the morning, his soft spot for expensive restaurants and for fine wine. So many small and big things! Whatever could fit in ten full, lively, passionate years.*

*He also knew about you, Michalis, my Greek love. This was your nickname. He had found amidst my personal belongings, a photo of us. Summer, on an island and two sunburnt children who are staring, smiling and clueless, at the camera. That selfie is the sole souvenir of that passion. A photo and a pile of letters containing a precious de profundis confession that I preferred to hide in a deposit box.*

CHAPTER 3

# PARALYZED

*Never before had the end seemed so remote. Everything up until then ended easily and the end was like a given, predicted. Only now at 20 something her university affair was similar to the strange nightmares in which one runs chased by someone or by something never encountered before, yet he is stuck. For me at least, this is how the story evolved. It was as if I had found myself at the edge of a dead-end from which you could only jump up to the sidewalk across the street, which however seemed to me to be located too far away! I was sitting there at the edge of the road looking at the passengers who were crossing. For some of them this jump was an ordinary jump. Others, on the other hand, seemed afraid at first, but in the end, they made the jump. In the end, everyone left. Only I didn't move staying in the same place, a petrified fairy desperate for survival.*

*I was looking for something seductive on the other side of the river, a hand that could pull me, something after all. To no avail though! The flow of the events kept going, the same, without any change and as for me, I always remained there. Day in day out more disappointed, more lost. In that dull place, where I looked dumped, I was invited in friends' commencements, in marriages, in baptisms, in funerals...I was standing, I was reflecting, and I was stagnating.*

*No doubt, I wanted to escape from that misery. That misery that only existed inside my head, according to your argument. A misery, that nevertheless you were the only one that could make me escape from. I wanted you by my side! I wanted your love close to me, your face, your hands, your breath. I had told you. But once more you didn't understand. As for me, I justified you once more. You were busy, you couldn't be next to me. You had engagements, bills to pay, audio recordings, rehearsals, interviews, and ignorance. You were taken as a given that when someone has exams to pass, he's got to be in a mood for study. You could not justify defeatism, insecurity, solitude, the fatigue of so many years in solitude on papers and books. You could not imagine how is this possible for people to do things they don't love!*

*I miss you I was telling you. All I need is to share with you the same space. Show me that you love me! Call me! Make me feel that I am worth something for you! Don't be isolated in your own world! Try to know my own world! Share your life with mine, this is the definition of the couple! You don't help me by telling me that it's simply my own affair and that I need to cope with it myself."*

*"I still wonder why I did not quit then. It was not that I was afraid to remain alone. Nor that I was afraid that I could not find someone else. I simply could not think of anybody apart from you, me and our relationship. I was severely annoyed by the fact that you seemed not to have the same need for my presence. There were times when I was almost sure that you were not the man of my life. A torturous back and forth of reflections with no ending. In other words, I was living in my misery while watching my life flying by. I never figured out if that kind of darkness that you suffocate in due to the absence of a beloved person, is what we finally call love, but let's face it, no one deserves to suffer for him with melancholia. It might sound tough, not a single trace of emotionalism, however, you babe would call it realism."*

*Reality, however, is not always that bad. The moment will come when the telephone rings and you will feel again that the entire world is yours and all these wonderful things belong to you! Because of him! The most important thing is for the negativity not to nestle inside you. Kalypso, from a mythic creature in a fiery look, had been transformed into and animal running to all directions, hunted by an invisible enemy.*

*--How are you doing, sweetie, will you be able to come on the weekend? I have a big performance and I would love to have you with me to get to know the other buddies.*

*--Yes, of course, I will come! I will be there on Friday evening.*

*She hangs up and she knows that she should not leave because she has a course exam on Tuesday. She also knows that she does not have enough money and therefore she will need to borrow money again from Alexandra. She knows that she has to go to Athen's incognito, because she has promised her parents that she will not go to Athens before she finishes her exam period.*

*She is aware of all these things, but her mind is already in the mood of Friday. And she arrives impatient thanks with money she has borrowed, and she cannot see him because they decided to continue their rehearsal and thus, she was left in her new coat that her mother bought from the best store in Larissa and set it to her as a gift in the darkness of the theatre. Sometime the rehearsal ends, and he approaches her with love, but she is ready to grab him by the neck.*

*--Sweetie, come to introduce you to Mr. X.*

*(Mr. X. is perhaps the biggest name in Modern Greek music!)*

*--Mr. X., THIS IS Kalypso, my sweetheart.*

*--Nice to meet you, I am clumsily whispering trying to grasp the truth in his words.*

*Yet the disarming sincerity of his eyes does not leave her any opportunity to contest the truth of his words. And while she was ready to burst out, she embraces him and keeps silent. She is introduced to the other members of the band with their girlfriends, they go for a drink, but she still feels that she does not belong to their group. Her life is so different from theirs and so boring!*

*--I can't understand what seizes you when we are with my own people. You behave like a person with disabilities. What's the problem? That we are university dropouts? He asks her in indignation on their way home.*

*--I don't understand what you are saying! You know very well how much I admire you, both you and your friends. Simply, I have nothing to share with them, she replies in a effort to justify her behavior.*

*--Of course, you don't have anything to share, since you go and hide yourself in a corner and you observe from above everyone like a diva.*

*--You are unjust. And ungrateful! For I myself once again I changed my schedule in order to be next to you.*

*--You should not have changed it then! He cries indignantly and every effort of reconciliation is destroyed. All anticipation for these magic days is gone...*

*They go up to the apartment and go to bed. She should have preferred to have left, but where to go at night? She hugs him and apologizes without knowing why. Perhaps simply because silence scares her.*

*You understood well and were perfectly handling the situation. When your little girl is not in the right mood, it is much better if you don't say a word, to let her calm down and after ten minutes at the most, she'll show up to say sorry since she has a big need to love her. Notwithstanding the reliability of this technique, I was always afraid that you would feel bored of me and my winning. Whenever though "this thing" was alive I could not help myself confronting it. Or perhaps, I was not trying enough. I believed the same as you believed that there would be a moment that "this thing" would change. As I grow older, I will be capable of controlling my spontaneity better.*

*A day came when Calypso grew old enough and gradually using more often her second name. She became more down to earth, more easily approachable, and happier. In addition to that, Americans could much easily pronounce Vasiliki. However, he was not next to her to enjoy her mature face, now that she was rarely using any more hysterical behavior, moodiness and unreasonable winnings. Time has changed them both. Whatever brought them close, it has separated them. They were two kids, offspring of Icarus who got in flames and didn't have the chance to become Daedalus. As the details were hidden in the back drawers of memory after all these years, perhaps it is her imagination which has altered their relationship in a unique love and nothing more existed but a beautiful love.*

*Oblivion, the ultimate protection, a kind of protection even toward itself. As years pass by, words get dissolved in the infinite, the pauses, the expressions, the dreams. It only remains an image of an abstract painting, where it is of no importance to discover what it depicts, but only what emotions are generated in its view. Her life is loaded with such paintings, from her parents, siblings, friends, spouses, lovers. Loaded with nostalgia, sadness, inspiration, calmness, and productivity.*

*My friends! Thank God they exist and always had existed. But still, how much could you share with them? Let's say that you tell them everything! How realistic could their reception be? And how deeply could they know a situation which they've only heard it as a story, sometimes out of curiosity? I am wondering how well friends can know you? Of course, the good news is that they exist next to you when you need them, and they want to listen to you.*

*As for that, she was lucky. Calypso belonged to those people who were covered with a beautiful and sweet aura that attracts the others without reason. She always had people who proved to be real friends. Back then during the university years she had Alexandra, Andreas, George, and Zoe. Those were the basics and the best. During her passage from her first life, she met many people. Some became her friends for a while. Later on, even if they did not change their stance completely, they simply faded out and were lost. Others remained good people we happened to know while others were crossed out. These four friends, however, had seen a remarkable shine to reside in her during her relationship with Mihalis. They could see this special shine of hers which eventually disappeared when they got separated. The most interesting thing is that George and Zoe didn't have the chance to meet with Mihalis. They lived the one side of the type of firework type of love which eventually burst into flames within a few months and that in a spectacular way.*

*Andreas and Alexandra knew each other well before she entered their lives apparently to become a love triangle. Kids of immigrants in Germany. They left Greece searching a better future, they worked hard and survived an intense racist environment and for an unfounded reason they decided to support their kids' future in the country that dismissed them. With the German Marc super strong during those days, they offered their kids an enviable standard of living. Without, however, the necessary foundations so they could evaluate all those sacrifices which had been made for them. Alexandra was taking many things for granted, but she had a loving heart. A bit irascible, although sometimes it turned out to be for their own benefit. Andreas, on the other hand, was driving them crazy with his persistence on following rules and cleanliness, someone, after all had to be like that. To keep them not shamed and to be in good terms with the little all ladies in the building who were complaining about the noise. Yorgos and Zoe were a couple. At least there is some good news in all this story. They are still together. She baptized one of their kids thanks to the Internet again. They located her at some edge of the world where she was living at that time, and they made arrangements about the baptism. She hasn't seen them for quite a long time now, but they still keep a minimal communication. As if she could escape Yorgos! He would be furious!*

*When she left for America, everyone believed that she would return in a year the maximum. "This country is not meant for you" they would say to her. One should not forget that time coincided with a period during which the feelings of the Greeks were not the friendliest towards the Americans. "Americans, killers of peoples" various student-fathers who had acquired a PhD. in poster hanging would shout. Along with them other naïve people who, like parrots were reiterating the various conspiracy theories against Greece. The years passed by and while the world was changing dramatically, those people continued to tell by heart like parrots all these obsolete theories.*

*In her friends' case, simply they knew that she would not find the desired peace of mind in the foreign country. She herself knew it as well. But at that time, she thought it was the only solution. They would say whatever they would say simply because they thought that Michalis was the true reason for her departure. They never learned the true cause. They hated him because he had turned her life upside down, yet as if there existed a kind of tacit agreement between them, no one would mention anything. Perhaps they knew that any mention of his name would eventually bring tears to her eyes, hysteria, screaming, bad words. They didn't know, however, that her tears were for him who left for the country of the absolute silence. Bad words exchanged with Alexandra, obviously for other reasons. Eventually, however, no matter how wild their quarrels were, always a rainbow would appear to sweep them with its wonder. George, on the other hand, might not curse, but if he disliked something, although it was taking some time, he would reveal it at the end. He might have taken the winning expression of a kid, but his words sometimes turned out to be painful. Andreas was the resting potential of the group. He never quarreled with him, although there were times, he received his words. Perhaps in a handful of occasions he increased a little his voice. But that was all. He always believed that there was something in his grey-blue eyes, no one or at least no one could interpret. Now she knows well that there existed something in them. A "something" quite important and big, that it's a question how could be kept only inside his eyes.*

*Eyes like Zoe's are not found often. One might wonder how they look like after all these years, back then they were tremendously sensual. It would suffice a single eye contact to start dreaming. Black slanted huge eyes full with the mystery of the late night. A sadness which might have been the result of a maturity, authentic and pure at the same time, without keeping any secrets and hidden "things." Zoe was, initially for her, George's girlfriend. A person she had to accept from the moment he became part of her life. The initial courteous "I have to," took the form of "I want to" only to be transformed into "it exists." True, eventually Zoe became necessary to her own life. After long nights of talks, afternoons with coffees and early gotten up mornings she had to exist in her life. She was the exact opposite of Alexandra. One was calm, the other was stormy. One was patient while the other was revolutionary. One was born to be the classic type of the woman comrade, while the other was the comrade of the rebels. The one was holding the record of five words per minute, while the other one hundren words per second. However, both of them were with huge black eyes, from which you could not escape. Both loved each other. Both were present when one was in need of the other, although each in her own way.*

*"Loved one." Such a beautiful word! Tender, warm, intimate. A word that makes you feel so special, something like a princess, a mermaid, as if you are wrapped in a warm hug...*

*"How is everything loved one," you usually said on a phone call. And at the end, "Tomorrow again. Goodnight, my princess."*

*And then the silence. And reflection! Apparently, the world was not nailed yet by data and messages. It was the era a little before cell phones when the love game was differently executed. There were times when the future seemed so far away. At the same time, however, the phone call early in the morning is so special. She believed, crazy as she was, that one night's power would be enough to separate them. Like that, without any reason. Just because they would not have been embraced.*

*Often, I wondered what special your part really had, and I wanted like mad to come to you? I had no answer. I started panic-stricken to do steps backwards. I did not turn back. I was looking at you, as I was walking away from you, and I was wondering whether you felt anything.*

*"- I don't have time for thinking" he used to say. And she could not believe it. She knew however that if she could spend her energy otherwise, away from her thoughts fixed on him, she would have felt less unhappy. And each time she would become lost in her thoughts in various bad scenarios, something else would happen to awaken her from her torpor. Yet not that strong to keep her balanced. She longed to speak to her parents and seek their advice. To get their help and understand what was happening to her for the first time. Yet no such thing happened no matter how much she hoped for it. Her parents had started their own attack on her, because they did not approve of that relationship. The more they pressed her, the more she was attached to him. She started*

*processing various schemes in her mind so that she could spend as much time as possible with him. He, on the other hand, was not ready to undertake such responsibilities.*

*The sudden death however of a young beloved person is something that is able to take you out of the torpor. She was not a close friend. She was the sister of a close friend of hers. And she was young. And she was pretty. At the dawn of her life. She saw her for the last time during that summer suntanned and smiling. She kissed her, she asked her how everything was going. A beautiful smile and strangely tanned skin. That was it. The last image. Two days later an acute pain and then a test. And after that one more and again one more. The diagnose, pancreatic cancer. Maximum life expectancy, some months. No hope. She faded fast. She slipped from the beloved hands, like water. She flew for the "other" world leaving behind only pain and questions. She could not go to the funeral; it was exam period.*

*I still cannot explain it, but usually all bad things were taking place during the exam periods. As if the already existing misery was triggering even more misery. As for me, I was not a person with enough resistance and good planning. Nor did I have next to me people who were capable and willing to hold me during my slump and save me from my intense tendency toward self-destruction. To my big sorrow, I now realize that my course during some periods of my life was completely wrong.*

*There were other times, when my happiness was reaching the top of heaven—as that happened indeed sometimes— when plenty of people were hurting me with their judgements and ideas in their efforts to protect me. Always suspicious and disbelievers over my own decisions, they were finding the way to poison even my best moments. I try to remember how negative my friends were when I talked to them about you and how harsh they behaved when we separated. Our relationship was not suitable for me, and I was charged with our separation as if it was my personal failure.*

*I am wondering how much easier my life could have been if I could act like a moron or if indeed, I had been one. Above all I would have less expectations of myself. As for the others, I can imagine myself happy as I would receive whatever I wished. My wishes would have been easy for someone to offer. Perhaps I was the one losing the game, as I was always considering myself important and different. My controversies, my restless spirit and the sad smile that made me different from the others and irresistible, were always leaving me at the end, apart from the flatteries, with a widespread sadness and a rooted insecurity that in the long run I would remain sole. It is true, however, that I wished to relax and learn to appreciate the modest things in life.*

*No one, however, talked to her about these. Her parents were demanding from her the difficult stuff. Friends were so demanding and pressing that they were finally destroying the simplicity of the moments. As for the lovers, all injured by her own insecurity, tried hard to invent something unusual and different, capable of drawing her attention. By no means the word is about a total absorption of her attention, only about a momentary reward, which she easily offered them. Likewise, they themselves equally easily they would see how quickly the shining of her eyes faded away. She felt it yet she did not make any effort to pretend she was happy regardless of how good she was at lying. At times really difficult, she had convinced people who seemed, and perhaps they seemed intransigent and tough, without any trace of sentimentality. She was able to disorient even Alexandra, who always thought of herself to be very clever and shrewd. For her own sake. Until today, after the interval of so many years, the secret has been kept well hidden. She went so far away in order to protect her. Letting aside any indiscrete or simply strange question, America was not the place for the realization of her dreams. It was simply the ideal refuge from the life the others had decided for her.*

CHAPTER 4

# RE-CHARGED

*"Whom will you have by your side when you grow old? Who will bring you a glass of water? As for us, we will no longer be alive so that we can listen to your complaints. My daughter, your youth goes by, you will leave your last breath alone like the stray dog in a vine! My God, I will no longer be around to see your mess! However, you are my child, the lord still ties us together".*

*These words and all that jazz my mother shouted to my wrecked 22-year-old skeletal body. And in all that madness, she believed that my life had been really done and that all her Cassandra-like prophesies would very soon prove to be true.*

*Of course, being a dog and dying in a vineyard properly maintained, blessed with juicy dark red grapes, during a night of the month of August, due to old age and not poor, is not indeed such a terrible thing to happen. It's much worse to be human, to remain in the midst of the summer inside a room, to prepare yourself for the exam period and run out of time in your preparation, to be close to the time of graduation yet to have so many courses to pass and on top of that to expect a phone call that with all mathematical precision will never happen.*

*I had to live far away to see things clearer. I also had to learn to see the dark side of the moon. To face everything holistically. To learn that in life there is not only black and white, but many shades of grey. To learn to enjoy the value of silence. To learn to forgive. To learn to love myself. To understand that in a relationship there are no sacrifices and victims, but simple mortals who do not have all the answers and despite all their decent efforts, mistakes always happen.*

*And when you believe that the world has collapsed, at that precise moment, a strong hand appears to bring you back on the surface. Your breath again and you enjoy the fact that you are still alive. You begin to realize little by little the power and the enchantment of your twenty-two years. You understand that when you decide to use the gifts of your youth, you can reach every goal of yours.*

*Orestes appeared in her life when Michalis started thinking of the separation. When Orestes was talking, she felt she was reborn. His words sufficed to awaken her and make her realize that what she was experiencing with Michalis was sickening. Her rebirth was exclusively his accomplishment and she herself his sole creation. And as usually happens in similar cases, creation becomes dependent of its creator. It looks like it breathes through the creator's breaths. Like a baby united with its mother by the umbilical cord. Absolutely dependent, seemingly complete yet so precarious. Not even for a moment she did not think that she was going to correct a previous mistake by committing a new bigger mistake. All such relationships are defined by intense passion. A passion so powerful and so debilitating that it cuts your appetite off, it takes your breath away, stops your thinking. A passion that brings uneasiness, wakes you up at night with eyes full of tears, fills your mind with dreams, pushes you to do things that you have never before imagined. To run behind his car like a little tramp, to search for his home to leave him a message. To abandon yourself in the forgetfulness of the alcohol not to think. And when passion is forbidden, then it becomes even stronger. Stronger and more difficult to tamed. But it is also bothersome for the people around you.*

*"It is too early, my love, in this world to talk about you and me" he used to say to me smiling."*

*Ignoring the social outcry, she was convinced --that time of great naivete- that love can change the world, that it can light the way for people to freedom. What a mistake! People's mentality changes so slowly as slow as slowly the sun sets in Antarctica. Does it ever set? Even such a strong love is not enough to initiate faster procedures. More likely she risks being suffocated by people's wickedness. To them no such thing happened.*

*It's really scary how much power a single moment can have. You wake up and your biggest problem is whether the light jeans you wear make you look fat and you answer the first phone call of the day, and your life is changed forever. Within seconds you become a different person, your path takes a different turn. How weak we are in the sovereignty of moments! Nothing is ultimately in our hands. Everything is simply a matter of luck or misfortune. Perhaps we are not responsible for anything. Perhaps Orestes might have been right.*

*The important thing is that the two of them time ran out of time early. Everything ended suddenly. So unexpectedly that all seemed like an elaborate hoax. She thought that at any moment he would come again to her house, and they would start to talk. But he never came back! And she lost control of the situation. A creature without the creator resembles an abandoned baby. And worst of all, it appears when those who want to take responsibility appear. They take its life little by little up to their hands and at this point everything starts to get con-*

*fused. The truth, the lies, the known, the unknown, the perpe-
trators, the victims, the innocent, the guilty. There, in all this
vortex one begins to think differently. To give importance to
things that until then seemed unimportant.*

*There are some events that whenever they occur you won't
be able to overcome. No matter what. No matter how coolly
you think about them. Like the day she's learnt about Alexandra's love. For sure it was a test for nerves. Until that day
she had never talked to her about any man. She was so negative on such conversations that she initially thought that it
was not among her preferences. Always negative and sole.
As if she was afraid of something. Always with a strong tendency to de-construct the male gender. Always willing to rid-
icule anybody who has fallen in love. A suspicion always lurking for every single thing which had to do with love, something which made even someone with a strong character doubt.
As for her, she never was a strong character. Nor that Alexandra was particularly beautiful. That, however, was not what
made her unattractive to the opposite gender. Perhaps being
a little overweight, plus her efforts not to look sexy, were enough
to reach her goals. Distance. She believed that only by keeping herself on a distance would provide her with safety. She
had been right. It's just that some people are not in good terms
with others of the opposite gender. It seems for them difficult
to communicate. As if they represent a different species. It's
not whimsical, just a particularity.*

*All the above were true for Alexandra. At an instance during
their student era, it was circulating that they were a couple.
They did not pay any attention to it. Just laughing at people's
stupidity. They too were feeding these rumors. Something dif-*

*ferent was also present in their own behavior. Even if that happened unconsciously. Always together, sometimes holding hands, completely indifferent of the presence of same age boys, together in noon together in evenings, together in some nights. More than enough reasons to get misunderstood. She was with Mihalis, but as he was absent from her everyday life, he was only an image, only a conversation, and some weekends when nobody from her own environment had seen them. And all of a sudden Alexandra started functioning differently. First time ever. Like a woman.!*

*It was mid-October. They had class. They decided to step on and go, although it was not their habit. Isn't that a good thing about free education? Too much freedom. This remark was made for two reasons. They would be given the books and they would see the professor assigned for the class for the first time. There was also a small detail. The professor was a nice guy. That was the circulation rumor. Students had always some good words for him, something extremely rare. A true challenge then. Calypso had already noticed him from last year mainly for what he was saying, and he had made her a particular impression. A bunch of exaggerated theories which in her young brain sounded very attractive. She had talked to Alexandra about how much she had been impressed, however she had had cooled her down with all her caustic comments.*

*She told her how she was impressed with the serenity of his movements, the sound depth of his voice, the self-confidence which as derived from his words, the silver color of his hair, the small riddles over his eyes. His broken smile. She had told her about how much different love could be with a man so much older. She wanted so much to sense how much different is when you are fulfilled. When you have found answers to some of your burning questions. When your feet touch stably on the ground and the wind cannot push you here and there. She wanted so much to discover what exists on the other side. She hoped that she could have a look on her life twenty years later. What if this mature man could have the answers on her questions she was struggling with? What if he could strengthen her lame self-confidence and provide her with the power to follow her heart? Could he love her enough so that he could help her achieve the ultimate goal? Could it be possible that this would lead to a balanced relationship, or she was simply looking for another paternal figure who could also be her lover?*

*Orestes was not married. He was very often mingling with his students. He was human, approachable, and ready to help each time a student might have been "lost" and was seeking his help. Whatever was involved with him was so different from all the other professors. That was an oasis in the boredom emitting from the academic life.*

*There were, however, lots of things from his personal life that Calypso was ignoring when she was building scenarios in her mind. For instance, she did not know that he got married in the past and this marriage lasted less than a year. She did not know that his wife abandoned him while she was pregnant and since then he had never seen his child a single time. She did not know that for years now he was not talking to his parents. She did not know that he did not have any friends outside the university. She did not know that he had numerous transitory adventures with women of the night. She did not have any idea about all this. The only image she could discern was the one that he had carefully crafted all these years.*

*The fact that he was not on such good terms with his colleagues was indicative. She naively believed that they were simply jealous of his popularity and because he was different.*

*No matter how hard he tried to attract Alexandra's curiosity and continue the conversation, the episode ended, and life kept going full of other thrills. When she saw him again that day, she noticed that in Alexandra's eyes something had changed. She was happily surprised, but she did not give any further notice. Besides, nothing exciting happened that first day. They joked, they heard him say some crazy stuff for one more time, they took the appropriate book, signed up their attendance and went for the necessary coffee of another day of student life. No one, not even a genius, would be capable of imagining how much their life would change during the coffee time on the student hunt. It was another routine, student, quotidian, process, however, with such an unforeseen sequel.*

*Books under their armpits they showed up in the noisy haunt, perhaps the only place always full and searched for a table. It was rushing hour, completely packed. They had caffeine cravings, same for talking. Especially for Alexandra who almost fought with a party to claim the same table. They finally took the coffee and left for an amphitheater. An empty one obviously! Amphitheaters don't have rush hours, the smoked a cigarette, Calypso rushed to the public phone when she saw it empty—her parents had blocked the outgoing calls since they had paid loads of money—to tell him the first good morning, I love you and that he wanted to meet the sooner possible, and then rushed after Alexandra.*

*She was not telling jokes that day, nor did she commented on all these left-behind ones who were surrounding us. She was lost into her own thoughts! Frowned, with somber expression and a gaze as if stuck somewhere else. I waited for her to start talking first. I didn't want to annoy her with questions, nor did I want to show her how visible was what happened to her. You had been in love, honey! And even at first sight. The only thing left was to realize it and admit it. Obviously, later, the love Golgotha would start. Let alone, unfulfilled love! But you were completely unprepared for what would come next.*

*What a guy, she said, and her gaze changed all of a sudden. She calmed down! And kept saying:*

*He is the man. Don't you think?*

*Unfortunately, Calypso also supports Alexandra's view. And it was not only his countenance which had thrilled her. It was his words, the way that he was unravelling his thought, his serenity in his movements, the security deriving from his age, his tone rather snobby. She was seeing on him all those Mihalis was deprived of. The unavoidable comparison resulted in Mihalis's dethronement, from the throne on which she had herself placed him. Or perhaps she was only willing to find someone who had the time to talk to her and she found in his face the opportunity to satisfy her wishes.*

*And now, after all these years, she figured out that for a young female student to become impressed by her professor who happened to be a bachelor and with innovative ideas, is a rather natural thing not to mention that it has happened many times. Back then, however, it was completely different. She had no idea. She thought that what she was into was so unique! She was creating stories which were far from reality.*

*Things were not exactly the same for Alexandra who fell in love for the first time. That morning she heard her for the first time talking with sexual innuendos. She was listening to her and simply could not believe that this fifty-year old man, without trying, made the impossible. To wake up her sedated female nature! Such a nature which had nothing to envy from any other. Their roles had been altered that day. Calypso was shocked and Alexandra was overwhelming her with erotic fantasies full of passion and creativity. How right are those who talk about love's miracles!*

*Same was her own renaissance about a year ago. A weekend with him and the miracle was there. She came back with an all-fresh smile and a different mood. It was the reason to see life optimistically. Without an effort he had given him power and self-confidence. At least at the beginning. Mornings were no longer boring. It was a challenge, and she was feeling ready for everything. Life was a beauty because he was part of her life. She was singing while walking, smiling to unknown people, she was not eating but she had a unique energy...even her studies were interesting. And she deeply loved him!*

*"I wanted to fly, to take something from the stars' shine, the moon's serenity, the sun's power, the sea's aura, the beauty of the blossomed meadows, the freshness of the mountain air...Only to be loved by him. To find me unique! To admire me! To keep him close to me. It's been almost twenty days we haven't seen each other, he is missing out on a tour abroad", I was writing in one of those precious soul consoling in an effort to sooth down my sorrow.*

*As Andreas was the one who had spotted them, he had real-*

*ized that there was something special lurking in the atmosphere and during the time Calypso was lost in her thoughts, he managed to pull out Alexandra's secret. Andreas was the last of the circle. From now on no one could learn something extra. Only if Alexandra wanted to. The question which was all over their heads was for how long her female nature would remain alive. Perhaps the entire story would be forgotten after the end of the coffee. But what if it wasn't?*

*Andreas worried passed from Calypso's house. They sat on the porch, they drank wine, from the one you cannot even smell, she told him one more time how much she was in love with Mihalis, how much she missed him, how much she enjoyed his different world and unfolded her insecurity, only to calm her down, telling her that she was exaggerating, reminding her nevertheless that the exam period was approaching and it was not a good idea to neglect it. After that Alexandra's issue surfaced and the dawn found them creating scenarios. It was as if they had come to know a different person. Absolutely justified that they knew nothing about her from now on.*

*Their concern was mostly based upon the scenario of rejection which seemed to be the most possible in case Alexandra decided to open up. Rejection hurts, especially if for someone is the first time. Sure, enough in this whole mess Calypso didn't have the slightest suspicion that she would end up being responsible for the creation of a love triangle. Perhaps, for the first time during this weird autumn night she reflected how much she would be attracted by the idea of such a relationship. Such a fantasy, no matter how intense might have been, flew over her eyes like a rustling and finally was forgotten.*

*Mihalis's absence made his presence intensely powerful. Almost of supernatural dimensions.*

*Andreas, before he left asked her to keep him posted. Alexandra didn't want to get bothered with questions. He told her to say hi to Mihalis, he asked her not to get too crazy, because she had already decided to leave with the first bus and disappeared in the fluffy atmosphere of the morning. For an additional time, she was altering her program in the last minute, she was leaving things unfinished, and she was going to meet him, because his absence was painful, and logic could not keep her far from him.*

*A dearest bus, making the already usual beloved itinerary, would bring her close to him. She would arrive next to him to tell him "Good morning" with a sweet kiss. This would give her the privilege to be the very first image of his day. She had omitted to ask him if his schedule was able to support her surprise. He twenty-year-old naiveté mixed with a general mentality, reflective of contemporary Greeks, made her to face the "schedule" with an intolerable and unjustified lightness. It took her a decade and a change of continent to realize how wrong she was thinking.*

*How much I came to love the buses during that period! They were conspiring in favor of our love and that made them unique. No matter how uncomfortable they were, no matter how awful music they were playing, or how slow they were moving, or crowded they were! They were bringing me straight in Athens! And the entire Athens was you!*

*I identified Athens with you, inside the music scene you were the only one who existed and unfortunately, all these resided in my soul for many years after our separation. There are times*

*I find myself searching in the artistic section of newspapers to find where you are playing, in the shops which sell records my eye always looks for the Greek rock scene and I imagine you passing by with your motorcycle, even if I am far from Athens. Mad stuff, perhaps even sick.*

*All these thoughts did not bother her mind that wonderful morning, when the only that counted was how to better create her surprise. She was not following the fluidity of the events. All these were completely irrelevant. In her own world, the idea of time was completely non-existent. Love nullifies time; it doesn't need it. All she needed was him. Indeed, blessed moments of unbelievable naiveté and uncontrollable egoism! One needs to live it at least once!*

*She arrived. She was passing from beloved places as she was approaching him. Shops, signs, buildings, streets, oil lamps lit, only for her, to lighten her way. So that she could easier and faster approach him. With flowers, freshly made chocolate croissants and love. She is outside his door. It's still early in the morning. She knows well that he is sleeping. She hopes he is sleeping alone. She can feel his warm breath under the blanket. She softly knocks at the door and even before he responds, she is already in, she embraces him, kisses him, nestle up on him like second skin and when finally, the door opens the only missing thing is the "I love you." He embraces her and pulls her together with her luggage on their bed. How hot! He undresses her, he kisses her, he relaxes her. He smiles! He whispers to her that she is completely nuts. Flowers on the floor, the croissants a little farther are cooling down, clothes lying all over them.*

*"I love you baby! How lovely you've come! All of a sudden..."*

*She looks at him as if it was the first time. He learns him from scratch. Twenty days on that age seem like an entire life. She feels in love with him even more now that she senses his warm skin on her.*

*I want him so much that I feel out of breath. I want to express to him so many things, but I am speechless. We embrace so tightly to become left in our love. And love covers our passion sweetly and gives birth to a beautiful love. I relax and accept you inside me tenderly and then we start. Our journey! All around senses of calmness, intensity, known, unknown. And everything is brand new. Different. I am lost, "ego" ceases to exist. There is no time, present, future. There exists only whatever I can sense. I exist only to desire you. I exist only to utter it to you. I transform myself to a carnal voice which vibrates, speaks, sighs. It struggles, in a constant flirtation with the limits…mine, yours.*

*And you whisper into my ear, "I love you." One, two, three, four, five, six, seven times… I cease to count. I don't question you. You say for the first time and although I want to scream out of happiness, I simply remain speechless and enjoy my small victory. For a few minutes only you're only mine. The voice, the smell, the passion, the warmth, your love…All mine! Calm and wild, romantic, and cynical, full of sweetness and orders, abuser, and victim, you carry me away. You pull me into a love game of contrasts which I sense for the first time. At first, I reacted. I talk, I ask you unrelated things, I laugh, I destroy the whole atmosphere. I struggle to keep alive my priceless individuality. You try, you don't give up easily. You try to tame me in a smart way. You uncover my veil of prudery, and you leave me nude. The female that you discovered inside me is now yours. Only yours. Completely yours. Ready to devour and get devoured. Ready to suffer, to give, to accept, and to chastise...*

*And the end arrives late, for sure. It arrives like a warm wave which plays on its wet bay. You make it to come and go, you play with me. You pull me, you tighten me like a string in the wind, you talk to me, you take me off...Today you take the lead. You prepare me and wait... It comes, I whisper with the voice that is left and then darkness covered with beautiful colors, muddy and strange sounds. You and me closely linked one with the other. I hold you powerfully as if I'm scared not to fall into the abyss.*

*"I love you", she tells him, and she tenderly kisses him at the tip of his eye. "I missed you", kid he tells her, and he tenderly embraces her.*

*He makes his body a nest, puts herself inside it, pulls the bed covers and like that they sleep embraced. Only for a while. Only for the time his engagements permit them. A phone call interrupts their sleep. He schedules a rehearsal. He knows well that easily the three hours can become four or five and like that their entire evening is gone. But she's come only for a night!*

*He puts the phone down and sweetly asks her if she'll join him. Obviously, she will! She came all the way to be next to him. What else she might do in a strange city for her, where she only knows his friends? Obviously, she will join him, because everything is a first-time experience for her. The studios, the rehearsals, the birth of a new piece, the inspiration. Because he is so handsome when he performs. She admires him, she adores him! She is proud to be with him.*

*Did I say it to you? I don't think I did. For sure I will join you even though I am indignant I live in your shadow. Even though I know how well it suits me to sing inside a studio. To be creative like you. You knew it.*

They keep sleeping for a little while until the phone's sound interrupts them again. This time it is definite. A female student of him. She always calls him to wake him up. To be on time at the lesson. She is 65 years old; he learns her guitar and he finds it hard to be on time for the lesson. She envies that lady. She envies her because she takes him away from her and because she still has the flame. She has only the one third of her years, she thinks she will never finish the university, she feels that she is short in willingness to do what she really wants to, she painfully experiences their love, perhaps losing the point and pretends that everything is fine in a life that is not fulfilling.

*You leave in a rush. Happy. You take it easy although you know that during the next eight hours you will do something that does not make you happy. You find something positive even in that. You jump on your motorcycle, and you go to earn your life. I reflect on how love changes colors when reality takes the place of desire. I sit on the bed which still has the smell of love, I pick up one of your CD and I feel that I am wasting my life. What am I doing here? For some time, I'll wait here, in a place that is not mine, a place without anything mine and I'll feel so miserable staring from your porch the faceless view of a city that scares me.*

*The phone will ring many times. I will hear the messages of all the people that will take you away from me, I will clean up a little bit, I will watch television, I will perhaps go to the closer minimarket for some cigarettes and chips and after that unable to go even for a walk, I will return home, go straight to the coach, then switch on the television to keep me some company till the time you will show up, then cry many times for the sacrifices I make for you, while you...This was the last time I cried for you while seated on that blue coach.*

*I was crying thinking that if I was with Orestes, he would never bring me in such a condition. He would have treated me more respectfully and understanding. He would appreciate my love and would return it. And as I was crying and thinking of Orestes, I felt that there was no reason for me to be on that blue coach. What I was feeling was not any more love. I had anger inside me. Anger and disappointment because you were not loving me the same way I did. And now while seating on your couch in your own house I am cheating on you. Perhaps only on the thoughts, but thoughts are more deeply rooted than the body. I am not crying any more. The end has arrived.*

*"Do you feel it?" I asked you.*

*"Perhaps." You replied dryly.*

*"Is it worth one more trial to save whatever exists?"*

*"I don't think so, Calypso. Soon we will find ourselves at the same spot we are in today. It isn't worth. Either for you or for me."*

*"But I am still in love with you. How can I give up the effort?"*

*"I am in love with you too, but it will lead nowhere. For every hour of happiness, we get numerous hours of solitude and pain. That's not how love is! If you love me, stay far, and do not mess up again in my life."*

*"Are these your last words?" I ask and I expect to hear no, but you make an affirmative gesture with your head.*

*That evening their gazes and words were like the cold winter mornings. Clear and desperately cold. He announced to her his decision to leave for America for the next five years. They both knew that it was their last night. She did not figure out if America was the reason or simply a dreadful coincidence. Besides, it did not matter. She proudly collected her rubble and left at the dawn. The flowers were still wrapped up in the paper on the kitchen counter. She could feel his gaze burning her back and touching the bottom of her heart while she was descending the steps as if she was drunk.*

*She found shelter in a taxi and left her tears to flow. She did not make any effort to control herself. And while she was living her first separation with wordless tears, he hears the taxi driver telling her: "Miss, I think a motorcycle is following us. Do you want me to stop or speed up?"*

*And as she was thinking that she was living the worst night of her life, everything became messed up again. She looks at the window and she cannot believe it is him. She does not know how to react and as the motorcycle approaches them, the taxi stops. She does not recollect having said anything. She does not recollect how she got out, how they embraced each other in the middle of the road with the motorcycle on the pavement. Unfortunately, whereas the scene was tremendously romantic, was not among those with a happy ending. It was the farewell's embrace. Embraced, they cried for their lost love until their tears froze up. He took her to the station. At the same station where some months ago fell her life was reborn. She entered the coach bus missing her steps as if she was drunk. It was the worst trip of her life till then.*

CHAPTER 5

# CHASED AGAIN

*If we could leave our lives to breathe and have the guts to live the fairy tale, our story would unfold in that way. Perfumed, like a calm body and relaxed which wakes up. But our unfinished nature, underprivileged from the very first moment of creation and cursed with an endless masochism, takes our hand and leads us toward the pathway of triviality. In that same old pathway, garnished with rose petals of security, order, measure, calmness…*

*However, me and you and him and her, all of us in a big voice were not looking for calmness. How would we like to live? Intensely, passionately, till we drop… Do you remember? And we were agreeing. In our eyes there was a healthy and warm red shine as a kid's drawing of the sun with yellow and orange, but what about after that? Where was it heading to? How many black holes were created from our ever lose little flames of our eyes? How many conversations we made for these fires, when sometimes crazy from the perfection of the inertia, we were feeling them to expand inside us and derail us from our everyday itineraries? Where have all these flames gone when we realized that they stole our future? How have we reacted when the world the way we knew it started collapsing? Did we ever sign in on Facebook and contested with a post on our wall? Sounds ridiculous, something like a painless hair removal. We hid on the back side of a computer monitor and we kept working toward our revolution passively.*

*However, the sleep fear is light. Its eyes are all black and huge, as it wakes up, they stare and paralyze us. Our feet stuck on the earth, our soul's wings shrink, and we have a single thought in our minds. Not even a thought. Unconscious reaction of defense. We slip inside us without any noise and in a cling of an eye like hard working bees we create honeycombs, walls, hoods, shells, electric wires, shields, anything that anyone can make. We hide ourselves from life itself, we refuse to accept our reactions, we hate ourselves who keeps feeling. However, all in vain! We play a game which we think we are in control of, simply because we are tough and empty of emotions, however, deep inside us we feel weakling all hurt and all being half.*

*I was leaving! I was up on a mountain, as I had imagined, and I was screaming. Both from happiness as well as from pain! I was proud of the little weakling inside me which had already taken the decision we were afraid of. I was winning my fear, their love, my dependence. I was leaving so that I could feel less pain, or perhaps to make them feel pain? Is that sudden running away of mine a redemption or a conviction? I couldn't know it, but during those moments I was not looking to soothe down this additional worry of mine.*

*I was leaving! And it was as if I had dived in a friendly, moist environment without any sounds, without threats. Warm and serene, as if inside a womb, out of mercy, being like an orphan, shrunk on the seat of an airplane which was taking me fast afar from whatever I loved most. I was punishing myself for not bearing love, the absolute form of compliance. I was punishing my soul because I was depriving it the shine of his eyes! I was punishing my mind because I had the desire to uproot from memory's repositories his voice, the words, the power of uplifting. I was punishing my body which desired him with all its remaining strength. I had to be punished because I was deeply in love! I was burnt! I was still burning!*

*She was feeling protected inside the airplane's belly and as long as it was cruising the sky with speed, she was relaxing. She was looking outside the small window and was admiring the beginning of the day. The alternations were intense, colors were numerous, alike but not the same. "We live in a multicolored planet," she thought and smiled lightly for the childish expression, which, however, was vividly depicting reality. A reality she was trying to escape, but at the same time it was making feel lucky to be alive and stare that wonderful sky. Numerous times she found herself staring at those birds made of steel which leave a white line, what a blessing would be to be inside them and leave afar. Perhaps this time someone else is staring and hoping for the same things, while she is the lucky one to leave for afar.*

*Some other times, mainly during summers, as I was lying on the beach and while immersing myself on the perfect blue of the sky, the white trace left by the airplanes bringing up new ideas. The white long line resembled the tail of the male sperm cell as if sliding into a blue, soft vagina, while a white-pink cloud would bump its way and get "fertilized." What could possibly become from such a union?*

*A beautiful lady pauses her delirium, in an effort to offer her some help. She stares at her and relaxes, the same way one relaxes when he stares at the clouds. She waits patiently for her answer, while wearing a continuous smile which keeps fading with time, while she thinks that if she was so beautiful, Mihalis could not live far from her. In her mind the scene of the last conversation left her voice disappearing. A hot wave begins in her uterus, arrives on her throat, make her cheeks red and mumbles:*

- *"Whisky soda."*

*She recognizes a small reaction on her gaze, as she opens and closes her perfectly painted eyelashes, after all it is only seven in the morning, but it is not her thing. Why should she care after all? How many people might have travelled by that plane in an effort to escape from something? And how many times she had discerned their internal struggle? She looks around, for the first time after they had taken off, in an effort to find in other people's gaze something that might reveal that others as well were at the same situation.*

*No matter how well she stared, however, nobody seemed to have a gaze full of anguish. Perhaps only the lady sitting next to her. She was also shrunk on her seat, a little pale and she had already taken two pills from the time they departed. Her hands are relaxing on her apron, locked, holding tightly a small bag. She is a nice-looking woman around sixty, I think. Her clothes match elegantly and seem expensive. Her hair is dyed with a warm blonde color, freshly combed in a helmet style. Why do all ladies over fifty, with only a few exceptions, have short haircuts and give them the same shape? She has beautiful fingers, or rather she used to have beautiful fingers! Time's effect on them is evident. No cosmetic cream is able to invert the shrinkage. Programmed cell decease. No one can escape. She wears her wedding ring together with a beautiful ring which attracts her attention and a classic women's watch, with a brown stripe. Without much thinking she finds herself observing her fingers. For sure they are in a better situation. No rings on them and no wedding ring to captivate her till now. It might never occur.*

*She secretly observes again the lady's hands, and she has the certitude that these hands that remain all this time at the same position will be welcomed by someone in London. Someone might need them. As for her, no one will wait for her in London, a trip she decided to go there last minute. Obviously, there is a friend who will accommodate her during the first time till things straighten up. That is not, however, the reason she decided to get headed there. Simply put, her budget did not permit her to proceed on a transatlantic trip the way she was planning. Nevertheless, for the rest she is heading to America. Some naïve people believed she was going to find Mihalis. She did not let them come and say bye-bye. She gathered her stuff and left in the dawn hours like a thief.*

*Whisky started already to act. She is tipsy and relaxed and forgets as she looks outside. Colors become vivid as time runs. Her tipsiness, however, increases and the only thing she expects is when sleep will kiss her eyelids. The transition from the state of reality to the dream starts suddenly and the borderline gets confused and while she hears everything around her, she is immersed in another world she cannot exit.*

*I open the door and enter an unknown room. It's dark and empty. I cannot see well. I proceed little by little with my hands open like antennas of an extra-terrestrial. I'm scared! I was always scared in the darkness. I suddenly touched some faces. Before I realize what's going on, these faces exit from darkness, as if they get out from the water and I can clearly see them. Alexandra, Mihalis, Andreas, Orestes, my mother...They approach and shape a circle. A circle which keeps tightening me more and more. They seem to be dancing all over me, but it is not a dance. No one smiles, no one talks, no one sings...They lead me to the door as they move slowly and tenderly as if they slide on a wet surface. They start mumbling something*

*I cannot hear clearly. They move faster, they almost jump. The floor recedes and I get lost in the vacuum. As I disappear in the chaos, I hear them screaming: "Leave, leave. leave..."*

*She emits a small cry and gets thrown from the seat. She trembles. Her fearful eyes look around to make sure everything is in order, her breathing is fast, and the lady sitting next to her is holding her hand and caressing her forehead. She gives her affectionately a glass of water, she recovers, she looks better and as she looks at her, she is ready to embrace her and burst into crying. Her pride makes her control her tears, she quietly thanks her and makes herself more comfortable on her seat. Uneasy she keeps staring at this woman and as she feels that unknown woman treating her so tenderly, she cannot anymore resist to the pain she feels and simply she releases it from her hands.*

*She covers her face inside her hands, but this won't let her escape from all those memories that led her to that trip. Their faces crystal clear like in the dream overwhelm her mind. They scare her. She feels that from one moment to another her mother will appear, she will take her from the protective of the unknown lady and she will pull her to the corridor screaming: "say the truth little bitch! You are responsible for everything! You have to pay! You cannot always escape and act like a penitent princess!" Mihalis will save her from her mania, he will comb and caress her hair, he will wipe her eyes and he will tenderly tell her: "Bye little guy! I hope to wish you'll be always looking forward my princess!" She looks at him stunned as he leaves away and although he feels abandoned both of them are full of love. Her mother observes with some irony the whole scene .and as she tries to put an order to the irrationality of the intense love, he arrives.*

*My sweet Orestes comes whispering that it is early in this world to speak for you and me.*

*She lets her words taken by the wind as she well knows that it's the only place where she can find him from now on. She feels his own sudden abandonment under the tough view of her mom who seems to be satisfied and all of a sudden Alexandra appears next to her. Crying, messy hair, scared, with huge black circles over her eyes, with her hands bleeding a little bit... "Don't abandon me, Calypso!" You tell me, and I search ways to help you, sweetie, but I have to leave.*

*She went away and she left her alone, to feel her own abandonment. She was not looking to punish her. Life has punished everybody in its own way. Herself, Mihalis and her mom and Orestes and Alexandra. No one escaped.*

*And that sweet lady, who through a number of coincidences brought her next to her during that trip, is not trying to escape. She stays there, she holds her hands and caresses with a fast movement the cheek. She is not judging her, nor does she tries to understand her. She only generously offers her calmness. She is not asking for more. This mute calmness suffices for her to escape. For the duration of the trip. She lets her calm down, but her eyes keep following here like a colorful kite's tail. Her voice sweet and warm like a withers sun ray, dissolves the mist of the embarrassment which almost suffocates them. "Do you feel better my girl?" What shoe could probably reply to her? How she could be sure if she feels better, since she doesn't even know if she is capable of feeling?*

*"I don't know if fear is better than pain. I simply felt scared now."*

*"Is it the flight?" says softly as if she does not want to understand her curiosity.*

*"I'm afraid I am coward! I'm afraid I am only leaving desperate people behind me, and I will disappear! I'm afraid I only give trouble to those who happen to know me! I'm afraid I will be alone!"*

*"I cannot believe that a sweet and young girl like you is capable to generate so much evil!" Her effort to light up the dark mood of the talk is slowly fading away as I respond to her sweet manners with a smile, like a tight string.*

*"See! Youth is not going hand in hand with purity."*

*Her answer is not satisfying her, and her curiosity suffers a sudden death, however, under a full control. She is not looking at her, her view is not accompanying her, sitting frowning, thinking perhaps that has channeled her tenderness of the wrong person. She lacks the courage to tell her "I am sorry." Lately she is living in a state of constant repentance. She feels tired. He does not want other apologies, other explanations, other truths! She desperately wants a lie. A nice, carefully chosen to lie to uplift her. Like a gentle floral quilt, laid carefully on the bed of the truth that creaks with pain and entangled truths.*

*The plane starts shaking vigorously. We are told not to worry, but who believes them? I lean backwards on the back seat, and I grab its handles. I think to myself that this may be my salvation. To get lost in the wind! The hand of my neighboring lady grabs my own tightly.*

*"-Sophia", she introduces herself with a voice that is struggling to pass the barrier of her teeth.*

*I wonder briefly why she tells me her name, especially at the moments we flirt with death, and I am thinking that if we ever crimp, certainly I will not survive to remember a lady named Sophia lying next to me. They will recognize us both if we are lucky, on the basis of a DNA analysis of our DNA of a tooth of ours, a bone, if any of these can be found. I am ready to burst out in nervous laughter, while I simultaneously feel that death does not particularly scare me, lest I don't feel pain.*

*The turbulence stops, -it seems that I am not destined to perish in the wind- Ms. Sophia takes her hand away and I am looking at London's lights approaching us menacingly. The landing procedure starts, my guts react and feel the same way when I am in love, and I expect my beloved one. Will I feel so again? I'm alive and I am thinking of love. Life finally has great strength.*

*"-Kalypso! Nice to meet you! "*

## CHAPTER 6

# FATE

*As a matter of fact, it is not so bad to arrive somewhere where no one is waiting for you. You feel calm! No rush to get out of the plane, not angry with the delay of your fellow travelers, not being worried about your luggage, not looking in the windows to check your appearance, not making plans for two. There is only you and yourself, a boundless freedom of movement and ahead of you an unknown yet hopeful future, if you think so. The time seems to acquire another dimension for people who travel alone. Shaw mind clear and virgin understands the new images differently. There is undoubtedly silence, but some things only in silence you are able to discover them.*

*The day is a typical London one. A crappy sunshine reminds that there's also the sun on the planet. Its existence nevertheless does not help you to make predictions for the moment. She only thought so because she wanted to begin her adjustment at least synchronically with time. For the first time in a long time, she feels that there is no point in silly chasing time, a chase to which she has submitted her life for so many years. Besides always time wins! She gives a glance at the clock but does not look at the time. She does it simply out of embarrassment, without a second thought. Mrs. Sophia, however, does not seem to share her personal views and embarrassments. While waiting for their luggage, she developed a hysterical relationship with the clock. She is counting the minutes, is doing calculations, thinking what to cook, wondering whether her beloved people will like the gifts she chose for them ... She is jealous of her even though she is infatuated with the idea of her absolute freedom.*

*She departs first and Kalypso is following her. The fibres of her mind are burning of curiosity to get to know the lover who waits for her. This little game puts her in a good mood for a while and hold her thought on a controlled level. She makes scenarios, hypotheses, she imagines ideal life partners, younger men, lovers of adventure and transient relationships. Enjoying her passage from the immaculate and fragrant corridors with the beautiful carpets of the Hethrow airport, she imagines Mrs. Sophia wearing black underwear and suspenders in a luxury hotel room in the company of her young lover experiencing passionate moments and endless real orgasms and she is a little bit saddened. For the very few orgasms she has felt thus far. She forges for a while her little game, because she is afraid that she will not look anymore for passion in her life. Passion blurred her judgment. She became a coward! Her pace becomes heavy, her good mood goes vapors. Where is she going? How duped was she to believe that a trip would suffice to erase her past? Perhaps they were right those who said that you have to remain in battlefield until the ultimate fall. When her partners were lost, she did not stay to complete the battle. To become a hero! She left fearful in order to escape the enemy. She did not seek honors, she only wished to live.*

*The clouds wearing black dresses gathered quickly and made a circle to dance. It is unbelievable how fast the clouds run in this country. They chased the lady sunshine away and started the party with many voices, drinks that flowed profusely and lights that endlessly flashed transforming the day into a bright night. She looks at the landscape out the window and longs already for the beautiful warm motherland.*

*Mrs. Sophia? She is standing tiptoe trying to recognize her head amidst the crowd. These days she is, quite ahead of herself, fast and proud. The little game of her mind, fortunately still alive, pushes her along with her cart towards her.*

*"Hey lady wait! How come not to see who is waiting for you? So many scenarios without sufficient answers?" Look at this guy, how young he is! Too young, in fact! Just half her age! Gee, he is so cute! It can't be... If he is her lover, I shouldn't get desperate. Life might reserve for her some nice surprises. She thinks that he stares at her. Wrong. She is the one stuck on them like a starving vulture. They don't look like a couple. They didn't kiss on the mouth; they don't seem to be in love. However, between them there is a bondage and a coziness. Like the one that matches all those who have disposed their body for the benefit of another. He hugs her from her waist, releases her from the stuff she carries, she keeps talking to him, she looks at him as if he is her entire world, she straightens his hair. They enter the subway. She enters into the same wagon. And the mystery is solved.*

*"Here is Calypso! Hi sweetie! Here is my son! Theseus, here is Calypso! We were sitting next to each other in the airplane."*

*Theseus and Calypso, what an exaggeration, one might expect Minotaur to enter the next station.*

*"Nice to meet you!" I say released and I prefer the image of Mrs. Sophia playing the role of mom, preparing food for her immigrated son and dearly sees him devouring it.*

*"Are you gonna stay long here?" the son asks him.*

*"No idea yet. We'll see! Each time a tiny step."*

*"We are exiting in a while. If you are in trouble, don't hesitate to give me a call. I've been in this situation, and I know how tough it is. Here's my card, any time."*

*"Yes, my little girl, don't be shy! My Theseus lives long time overseas. I'm sure he's capable of helping you," she caresses my cheek and focus as they become lost in their conversations. They disappear in the first station.*

*Her station is far away. She is melancholic. Underground travelling is a serious reason to get melancholic. There are some places on the ground, all grey and unknown, they barely differ from the underground ones. She feels that she might not be on good terms with that country. She's only been here moments, but she feels as if she belongs elsewhere. Where though? She wishes Mrs. Sofia had invited her for dinner, even okra, which she detests, would be OK. She hadn't eaten for two days now. She had forgotten it, but now she starves. Is there anything in Dido's house or she might keep feeding herself chocolates and corn flakes? Is she going to be thinned the way she remembers her? Her super-fast metabolism was getting to her nerves.*

*Dido was a friend from the old days. Schoolmates from kindergarten. However, I am much luckier. She was the kid of two parents who never considered themselves to be the perfect parents. They divorced when Dido was three years old. No traumas, no adapting problems…Only double vacation! And always a tendency toward not banning even her most crazy wishes. She abandoned the university during the first year. She figures out that the law school was not a match for her! She decided to study theater in London. And she went there. They did not meet often during these years but there was always an open line of communication even though they were not using it often.*

*When the events became more dramatic, she called her as she was the only one, she could talk to. She didn't tell the entire truth. She didn't give details. She didn't force her to learn more. She only told her that she didn't have any place to live and if she could live with her for a while, that would be the best ever gift she could have made her. Dido calmly responded:*

*Absolutely! Leave the melodrama! I've already told you so many times to come. I was not expecting you to produce a panic in order to come, but anyway. Come, so that I can see where the perfectly controlled creature has gone.*

*I'll be there in three days. That creature you remember died!*

*I'll be the judge on that. You are not in a position. Just try to take the right flight, from what I gather you'll easily board the plane from Libya and wondering how come London has so nice weather. Hugs, I'll be waiting for you!*

*Little Dido was waiting for her at the subway station. Skinny as she always had been. Rich hair all over giving an aura of a bygone era. She was in front of her white and warm like a little mom. Perhaps Mrs. Sofia might have been like her if she was left free to live without kids, responsibilities, family meals and husbands. Dido hugs her from her waist and leads her to her nest. She talks and talks, smiles, and flies. In the sky like a multi-colored balloon of helium. She has escaped but she is doing fine! For a few moments she feels that there are so many things that separate them! They are standing on different grounds. She knows her and she'll find them under her.... When she relaxes, she might be able to talk to her.*

*For the time being she keeps silent and enjoys her!*

CHAPTER 7

# LOVED SOFTLY

*Her nice grandma! Her savior! Without her to assist on her financial problem, her escape would not have happened. She did not interrogate her. She understood more than she could afford, and her urge made her arrive here.*

- *"Sweetie, you must leave for a while. Forget and be forgotten! Everything will be fine. Everything except death. You need to befriend him. It is not so difficult as you may think it is now. I bade farewell to many beloved ones, and I got accustomed to it. You'll never forget. You'll simply learn how to live in its shadow."*

- *"I lack the power grandma. I feel as if steamroller passed over me. Everything inside me got burnt. They got petrified! What have I done? The only thing I wanted in my life was to be happy!"*

- *"Kalypso, no lies to your dear grandma! You wanted everything and this is called arrogance. Hubris! It was not yet time for everything you sought to happen. Of course, now it does not matter. What happened, happened. No one can turn time backwards. Be courageous, my baby! Simply you were destined to grow up early!"*

- *"Grandma, I am scared! I can't believe that there will come ever a day when all this pain will be forgotten…"*

- *"No such day will ever come, my love! In very simple words, one day you will manage to put this pain in a little box of your mind, to lock it and hide its key for good."*

- *"Grandma, what would have done without you?"*

*- "You would have found the solution on your own! I's not that it needs great wisdom!"*

*Only to her grandmother did she bid farewell when she left. Her parents were still very angry with her. There was no reason for further explanations. So, thanks to her progressive grandmother with her thriller-like fairy tales and black-and white unbent logic, she was walking on the beautiful London pavements next to Dido. The neighborhood where they were living was considered "in" and it was very expensive. On a street nearby many celebrities from the show biz world had their residencies. She never met any of these people while she stayed there. Nevertheless, she was thrilled in the idea that her excrements were mingling with those by Sting in the same sewer system.*

*Crazy ideas like this one she was exchanging with Dido, the first night at her doll house that she shared with a couple, Alexia and Harry who were absent that first evening. Alexia had visited her girlfriends in Paris and Harry went to his parents for a family affair. Harry was British, Alexia a true Greek. The house was not small, yet everything in it gave the impression of a contrived freedom, something like a hat made her move cautiously. Dido's room must have been the smallest, but she had decorated it with great taste.*

*-We will be sleeping together, my dear friend! Is it ok with you? As for myself, I do not care at all, since you have become such an attractive girl!*

*-I don't care, because you have remained so thin like a tree branch and therefore you will not take much room.*

*She arranged her things wherever she could find space and*

*she offered Dido her presents. A box of Malboro lights and two bottles of whisky.*

*"I modestly buy my accommodation in your doll house straight from some fairy tale with these goods, your honor Leader Dido," I said making a bow.*

*"We are going to have some fun nights with all these here! Welcome my exhausted immigrant" said and took in her hug the bottles as if they were her two babies.*

*Are you hungry? I think of preparing Chinese!*

*Perfect!*

*If she only knew how much Chinese she would eat during her stay in London, she wouldn't have agreed in such a joy. "Just relax, I don't need any help. Take a shower to relax and keep your energy, since you've got so many things to tell me!"*

*She took a towel and entered the bathroom. In its one side the wall was inclined. You could stand up only in certain spots. She was usually taking her shower seat so there was nothing to bother with this weir's architecture. Such a nice thing when you don't need to switch on the water heaters and wait till the water heats up! No one risks getting stuck there in the cold water in case something goes wrong with the heaters.*

*She always loved to immerse herself in the water when she was sad. She was thinking that water could purify her brain from sad thoughts. Whereas the result this time might not have been completely satisfying, but perhaps this time is the particularity of sadness. She filled up the shower and sat. She slipped her body inside and let the water cover her up. Only her nose was out and as the water was flirting with her ears, it was chang-*

*ing the acoustics of her microenvironment. She had not tight-
ened the faucet very well and the falling water drops were
making a terrible sound. She spent some time relaxing in the
warm water but after seven slow breaths the relaxation started
to generate images in her mind, words, smells, and got up immediately. She quickly washed herself and exited as if she
had to go somewhere. She was standing in the small room
clean, tired, and starving. The Chinese smells coming from
the kitchen had widely opened her appetite. Little Dido was
waiting for her in the small kitchen where you could only
walk on the side with a glass of wine in her hand, with a candle
lit in its half, and ready to make a wish. Facing her warmth
and her care-free smile she almost froze. She felt an old powerless lady in front of her. How could she talk to her about
all the things which had happened! Was she able to understand or she would throw her into the fire?*

*She picked up the glass and responded to the smile.*

*"Welcome, my dear friend!" said with a meaning and knocked
her glass decisively.*

*"Nice to see you!" I said in a normal way, and I gave back the
smile.*

*"Come on, don't sit there like a statue! Try it and tell me how
it tastes. It's my specialty!"*

*Her taste buds reacted happily from the first mouthful.*

*"Fantastic!" I had the time to say and then I immersed my-
self in the job.*

*"Eh! Don't eat so fast! It's a heavy meal, loaded with
spices...You won't be able to sleep tonight!"*

*"My little Dido doesn't place in front of a starving one a piece of poetry! Cheers! You're an impeccable cook!"*

*After about ten cheers and another ten or so boastings, they got up from the table and laid on the couch for a cigarette to help digestion. As they were drinking the last glass of wine and were trying to shape little rings from the smoke of the cigarette, Dido suddenly threw the following words.*

*"Your parents know that you will live with me. They called me a little before you came. They did not know when exactly you would arrive. Did you escape or something?*

*Almost...Listen little Dido! Things are a bit complicated! I will explain everything to you when I can. For the time being, don't ask me!*

*OK! Your request has been accepted. And in order for the things to become a little relaxed I go straight to bring the magic plant.*

*Before even getting upset with her parents and their craze to follow everywhere in her steps, Dido returned with a small fuchsia velvet pouch, bound with a leather lace, and pulled out carefully the magic plant. A little later they were both lying back on the carpet and were laughing crazily as if drunk.*

CHAPTER 8

# LIFE INTERRUPTED

*Same music scale every single day. At exactly the same time he stands with some melancholy and uses the same music scale. Hoping that he will not play any false notes anywhere. Interpret his piece without a tiny mistake, this is his inner hope. Stuck with his dark tie seems to try to do the same in his life. Perfectly irones suit still having the smell of the local dry cleaner shop, which is right next to the Indian cuisine restaurant, covers his frail white skin and starts. He wants to fool people with his authentic behavior, to stress them to the limits with issues and deadlines and persuade them that errors are only for those who lose control. One wonders how come this fifty something man with the perfectly disciplines red hair, didn't figure out all these years that the perfect control is a first class of a loophole. Human eating and perfectly hidden.*

*During the first time in London, she spent many hours at home as she was not in the mood for anything else, she was just looking at other people's lives outside the window. Facebook was not part yet of their everyday lives. This fifty years old man had attracted her attention. First because he was living exactly across so he had a complete view of his life, and second, because he was so carefully controlled that he was turning on her nerves. He was also walking around all alone. She knew his schedule since it was the same old boring one. He was out of his home at 7:15, he was carrying the same fully loaded portfolio. He returned somewhere between half past seven and eight every night. He was belated due to his shopping at the supermarket. Like many English people he had the habit not to pull the curtains, and as a result she could invade his personal life. He was immediately changing his clothes and started cooking right away. He was rarely bringing ready-made food from outside, something common for bachelors.*

*After his meal he was sitting at the same armchair, which she might say was his loved beloved, and smoked his cigar drinking something alcohol containing, which, according to Dido—since she was also part of the spying when she was available—was a type of wine which is meant to be consumed as a dessert. He was always drinking one single glass. Later he would go upstairs where the sleeping room was located, and he would change clothes. At that point the immediate view was gone as the curtains were dark and always shut. Not that she wanted to, nevertheless! In a while he would come back wrapped up in a dark robe de chambre, holding a bunch of music scores. He was sitting on his piano and started playing with seriousness. He could sit there forever. There were cases when we were hanging out with Dido for a drink and when we were back, hours later we were finding him at the same place. The only thing she could not figure out was if she was playing the same piece.*

*The mystery was solved after the storming of the police. They were endless tapes on the same track recorded. From the first attempts until the last was almost perfect his playing. When they arrested him, they even found him sitting at the piano and playing calmly. He told them that he was willing to confess everything if they would sit and listen to him play, even briefly. During the warrant execution, he confessed them that he had killed all fifteen people who were working in his business, all carefully chosen by him to be bachelors and with all their relatives oversees. He told the police that he had killed them because the business was close to bankrupt, and those people were responsible for that. He also added that although he tried hard to cultivate them by putting on a daily basis the tapes with the recorded piece, not only they did not improve but they were also making fun of him behind his back, as when he was putting his music which he had to struggle to record every night, they were applying ear plugs in order to continue to work. As a result, within one year the business collapsed, he fired all of them and later he killed them.*

*No one had the curiosity to search for the lonely people working for him. He knew that no one would ever search for them if they disappeared one day. So, he was slicing them and burying them in his yard. All of them but the last one. Exactly like in the tales. So, when he fired the last one, he did not know that he was not living any more in his loneliness. When he visited him at home to give his compensation, he realized that he was living with a beautiful redhead girl who was playing the violin. It was for him impossible to kill someone who was living with a musician. On the other hand, however, he could not forgive the fact that somehow, he contributed to the failure of his entrepreneurship. So, he had to find a way no one would be treated unfairly. That night he gave him his compensation and guaranteed that he would find him a good job. He also invited them for dinner the next evening and asked the redhead to bring her violin with her to play something together if she didn't mind. Of course, she wouldn't mind, since he had promised them to find a job to her beloved one, he had saved them after all. If they relied on her earnings, that would mean some harsh days were to be expected in the future. Life is so difficult in London!*

*They made love at night and remained sleepless thinking the difficult days in the future would not arrive for them, all thanks to the generosity of the old boss. As for the boss, he walked a lot that night trying to find something fair for everyone or at least for the majority. He was waiting for them the next day, and everything seemed like a celebration. He had cooked, he had made a dessert, he had bought nice wines, he cleaned the house, he bought flowers, he made the piano shin, but in spite all these the house was emitting a strong smell of mausoleum. It was clear, he could see that himself. Same with her, as she was observing all this activity she felt dying out of curiosity. Lately she had ceased to observe him because she was out more often and because his life was dull. That night, however, she heard him dining in the yard with the young couple. She heard them talking, laughing, playing music. He was at the piano, and she was accompanying him with her violin. He was differently dressed, more casual, she was smiling, he was treating well his young visitors. She almost felt jealous. Since he so much liked music why didn't he invite her one time since he's seen her playing the guitar? Who could imagine that her guitar would be her lucky shield! The night was unravelling smoothly, and Calypso left their melodies to go to a party with Dido. At her school. All aspiring actors gathered. Unbearable! She was not so much in the mood.*

*Alexia and Harry had come at the house and since she was not meeting them at home due to their schedules, that party would be a could occasion to get to know them better. They were feeling awkward too among all these artists. Dido on the other side was shining. She was frolicking from one party to the other mixing up Greek, English, French, Italian, and perhaps German as well. She was happy to see her using her Mediterranean temperament with such dexterity. Even though the three of them pulled themselves aside whispering their stuff carefully, as if they did something wrong. After all, how many aspiring stars could that hall take in!*

*While getting back home their mood was happy, with slightly singing at the subway and teasing Dido for her enormous diva-like temperament she was hiding in her. Harry was not shy any more with Calypso and she particularly liked that. They were teasing and joking with each other. It was a beautiful evening. As they were arriving home, however, their knees started shivering. A crowd had gathered, sirens, lights. Fire fighters, Police, how come? They could not distinguish clearly yet. "There's no fire," someone observed.*

*They kept walking fast to make sure that nothing was going on at their house or at their friends from Yugoslavia who were living at the ground floor. Their fatigue, their sleepiness and their tipsy mood disappeared within a few minutes. They were finally standing at the sidewalk outside their house. That's where Zora was standing as well, who was clearly shocked as well. It was clear that something bad had happened at the house across. At the house where today they had a small gathering?*

*Did they steal him? Did they kill him? Had they been attacked by any unknowns? Speak, Zora!*

*Yes! It was a young couple. I saw them entering. She was redhead, she was holding the violin. As for the man? No, I didn't notice him, he did not have anything special. Yes, blonde, a typical Englishman. No, I don't remember if they've arrived by car. Does it matter? He attacked them!*

*Who?*

*Are they alive?*

*I called the police. I saw the girl been thrown from the second floor's window. I don't even want to think what would have happened have I had been even a little late to inform the police.*

*Is she alive?*

*I don't know! Next, I saw the door opening and the landlord rushing toward the girl with blood in his hands. He took her in his arms, and he kissed her. At the doorstep I also saw her companion. He was on the floor trying to make it to the exit. Blood everywhere! Police found the other guy stuck on the young lady. Then the ambulance came and took them, and Dayan is over there, answering police questions. I can't make it any longer, I'll go in. All the streets are full of blood. That odor makes me sick. I'll go in, are you coming?*

*They didn't say a word, they simply followed her. She opened the door, and all sneaked inside like starving baby dogs. No one wanted to be alone that night. She prepared tea for them, they all sat speechless over a table waiting for the moment there would be silence again. They were not looking outside. They sight was toward the door. After a while Dayan entered. He was a man of almost two meters long, but that night he looked small, skinny, and powerless. He took his coat and told them that he would go to the police station to answer questions. When leaving he thanked all of them for keeping company to Zora. "She shouldn't be alone these hours," said and he caressed her hair.*

*He left and with him the sounds of death left. Only a few police officers remained in order to continue the search. Their presence did not give them any more sense of safety. Harry decided to play the male to calm the female crowd down. He stood up and started making fried dough into small pies. He knew the whereabouts of the house because the couple had invited them many times for dinner.*

*-Are you sick? Alexia asked Zora, who seemed very pale.*

*-No, she answered smiling. I am pregnant and today is a bad day. Full of uneasiness.*

*--Pregnant! This is wonderful. An occasion for a party! When do you plan to disclose it to us? Dido asked her to pretend she was offended and turning to Harry, she said:*

*-Double the quantity, we are very hungry!*

*It was as if that unborn baby had magical powers and would dissolve immediately the cold death fog that had fallen on their neighborhood.*

*The fried dough small pies were unique, but their appetite was limited. They opened the sofa where Zora set herself comfortably and they slept on the floor. No one wanted to be alone that night. The slaughtering of the next door slipped like a heavy shadow through the big windows of the basement and at moments the odor of the blood mixed with ammonia hit their names, but the harmonic breaths of people appeased the clatter of Calypso's mind. At some point, she stopped resisting her torpor. Another murder in the same neighborhood the same night was improbable about happening again, she whispered in the air, and she closed her eyelashes tightly.*

*The next morning, I don't remember who woke up first. Most probably our eyelashes opened successively. Dejan had re-*

*turned and was sitting in the kitchen. He made coffee for everyone. He seemed as if he was waiting for us. To keep us up to date! Zora looked all-beautiful. Her worry had been gone. Her husband stood next to her and was holding her hand. Huge and strong. No one talked. We waited for Dejan to start talking. He started talking calmly.*

*"Both of them are alive. They had a very difficult night, but they survived. The girl underwent surgery and there is a risk that she is left handicapped. The man lost a lot of blood, and he is under shock. But they will survive. In the garden across from us special teams have been digging since morning. They have unearthed ten cadavers. They surmise that they used to be former employees of his. The one from yesterday was the last one he had laid off. He did not kill him directly because he was carried away by the young female musician. He himself was passionate about music. Especially classic music. They found many tapes in which he had recorded one and a single piece. He did not explain why he committed the murders. In yesterday's case, he had planned to murder the man and keep his fiancée as his permanent companion. In music and in all circumstances. He isolated her in the upper room, he locked her in and went down to get rid of the young man. She understood his intentions, and, in her desperation, she jumped out of the window. If she had not dared such a deed, today both of them would have been dead."*

*Thus, the enamored couple lived, Zora gave birth to twins, Dejan was awarded the medal of bravery and harry became a famous chef. As for the three of us, each one of us became very happy, rich, and successful in her career and in her personal life with many children.*

*Somehow like this the story would end if life were a fairy tale. But it isn't!*

*Zora delayed her phone call because of nausea and thus the police found the new couple slaughtered and the murdered playing his favorite piece on the piano. It was the first time he had played it impeccably. To the investigator, he said that all those enemies of the art had to be sacrificed in order for him to achieve the unreachable.*

CHAPTER 9

# GROWING UP

*When the odor of death approaches your own door, memo-ries awake. You cease, even for a moment, to circulate your flesh snootily all around and you think that you have no means of knowing when your life contract ends. The chills that go up and down in your spine remind you that if you will see the sunlight again, it is totally a matter of chance. Both your life and your death is a long chain of completely unde-termined coincidences.*

*The first period in London she considered the people like en-emies. She behaved coldly even to Alexia and Harry. She did not speak much, she did not eat much, she did not go out, she did not watch TV, she was always locked in her room sunken in a pile of books, most of which were of no interest to her. She was trying by all means to keep her mind busy. Dido showed her a lot of understanding. She was living with her without making her feel suffocated. She discreetly highlighted her pres-ence and patiently waited for the day she would decide to talk to her. She was trying to dissolve her worry each time she saw her smile with difficulty, but Calypso simply did not have the strength to react yet.*

*After the murder of the next door everything changed. Dido stopped trying to smile. She insisted on looking at her and waited to learn what made her leave like a fugitive. But nei-ther of the other roommates looked at her indifferently any-more. As if the murder of the next door had awakened their consciousness. She felt the grace period reached its end. She had to speak up, to reconcile with everything that had happened. To clarify within herself and to the others which her role was. To assume responsibility. Regardless of the consequences. Otherwise, she would not be able to carry her life further.*

*That day a beautiful sun made the city look different. People on the streets did not run. Instead, they were walking quietly enjoying the impeccable blue sky. Some of them had laid down on the fully green parks and spent peaceful moments before returning to their cannibalistic offices to complete the chores of the day. In such a park she found herself next to Dido. They laid down on the grass and with bitter joy she realized that for the first time after such a long time she actually did something. In Greece only in the summer she used to sunbathe on the sand. But on the grass, she had never sunbathed! She felt beautifully, peacefully. She was ready.*

*They both looked at the sky and silently longed for their country. Would they ever return?*

*-When do you plan to return? Dido started first.*

*-I don't know, I have not given it a thought… if however, I am a burden to you…*

*-I didn't mean this! With the University what are you going to do? I hope you don't quit… It's only one year left!*

*As a matter of fact, how much time theoretically is left before graduation has nothing to do with how many courses you must pass. One of the many and awkward mistakes of the Greek educational system.*

*-I don't think I can ever return there… I don't know, I will see.*

*-What are you saying, Calypso! This is nonsense!*

*Dido had lost her patience. And she continued:*

*-And what are you going to do? Will you begin something here, will you work? Sooner or later, you'll run out of money! Until when your grandma will sustain you? Her pension cannot stand up to the high cost of living in London!*

*--You can't understand, my dear Dido! Things are complicated. It is not that easy to take a plane and go to the University...*

*--Talk to me! I can't stand it anymore to hear for such a long time that things are complicated. You can't hide all your life! You get it, I imagine!*

*--You are right, simply, I don't know where to get started...*

*--It's not this, Calypso. For some reason, you are afraid that I'll throw all the blame on you. I will not do it! I only want to know what has happened, so that I can help you.*

*-I have pain! Words don't come out...*

*-They must, Calypso! You must decide what kind of life you want to live. Locking yourself to your silence, does it help you to ache less?*

*The situation did not allow for further postponement. I took a deep breath, and I opened Pandora's box.*

*-About Michalis, I have told you a few things, do you remember?*

*-Yes, the musician. What happened?*

*-We separated.*

*-Sure, I have understood that. Totally expected I would say though. This was not love, my dear girlfriend! It was torture! Each time we would talk, you were in deep misery! Anyway, let's proceed.*

*-You are right. Yet when I was with him, I was happy.*

*-Sure, ten days a year. Is that what you call a relationship?*

*-It doesn't matter anymore. He left for America.*

*-Safe travels to him! Is that why you are sad? There are also orange trees elsewhere that give oranges if you know what I mean! But what exactly does Michalis have to do with the entire story?*

*-I will explain it to you. It's not that simple. The complication started just a little before Michalis left for America. I met somebody else. Orestes.*

*-Ok. Parallel relationship. I see you're quite advanced...And moreover, you did not mourn a lot for your big love!*

*-Let me explain to you! She cried distraught, but deep down within herself she knew that Dido was right. And she continued. Orestes was a professor at the University. We had started classes three months before my separation from Michalis. He was a great guy! Cute, single, great teacher. Briefly speaking, he was the day's subject. Even my friend Alexandra whom I considered a lesbian, fell in love with him! The affair was kept between us in our own conversations, until the moment I visited him at his office to undertake a written project. I sat across from him, and we started talking. Everything about him was extraordinary. His eyes, his smile, his hands. But most of all, I liked the way he talked, that first day I spoke with him much more than I had spoken with Michalis the entire year I was*

with him. And I had missed him so much! One topic brought up another one and I started talking to him about Michalis and mainly to cry. I did not mention anything to Alexandra. Two days after, I stopped by his office. Without reason! I only wanted to see him and talk. After that meeting, many more followed both in and outside the university campus. We spent endless hours together! We sat and conversed for hours. He always had time and the will to listen to me.

-Sorry, so that I can understand you! You were... a normal couple?

-Oh, Dido, sex is not the only thing that ties you with someone! No, we did not do it, if you ask about this! And no, I would not say that we were a couple.

-Although it is hard to get it, where is the problem? Did Alexandra see you and you had a quarrel afterwards? Hm, what can we do? Platonic eros, Platonic eros... but you are also a good piece yourself!

-Dido, Orestes is not alive anymore.

It was the first time in a long time that she was talking about him.

-He died! And he died because of me! And Alexandra is in jail, also because of me!

-Hold on, Calypso! How is it possible that an innocent flirtation ended up so tragically? How did this happen? How did you spread around you all this panic?

Her words deep nail scratches within my heart.

-Probably because I was not sincere. To Alexandra I had not told anything about my regular meetings with Orestes. I know

*I should have told her, but he was mine and what we had built the two of us was so unique. I was in love with him. I did not want anyone or anything to interfere between us. She has crazy about him. On the one hand, I could not believe it and on the other I did not know how to manage her. She was my friend; I did not want to hurt her! I had told him about Alexandra. He did not give it any attention. He only smiled and told me not to worry. One evening Alexandra saw him kissing a girl. She did not realize that that girl was me. We were at the backyard of the school. Desert, winter and pitch dark. I left not to miss the bus and he went up to his office to get the keys of his car. Alexandra followed him. She was out of her mind. She lunged at his office screaming, she made a scene to him, they started fighting and during the fight, she pushed him, he lost his equilibrium and crashed into a steel globe. And he died. Instantaneously. Alexandra never learned that I was the girl he kissed.*

*-It was the first time we kissed each other, she said and looked Dido in the eyes waiting for her verdict.*

*-All this story sounds so far-stretched that it could be a film scenario, Dido said rather slatternly. And then, what happened with Alexandra?*

*-Eh... what do you think? She called 911 and turned herself to the Police. The trial followed. I appeared as a defense witness. I trembled not to reveal that I was the pretext for all this. I was forced to reveal the truth to my father, because he was Alexandra's attorney of defense and despite his efforts, Alexandra was sentenced to 15 years in jail. My father, at the moment of the verdict, whispered to my ear that he wished for my disappearance from now on and ran to support Alexandra and her parents. I am now learning that they are fighting*

*for a court appeal.*

*A long pause accompanies their glances.*

*-After all this, what is your opinion, will I ever be able to return?*

*What could Dido reply after such a cataclysmic confession? Besides her countenance betrayed everything. Suddenly little Dido ceased to be so cool and to consider everything simple. Everything was seen now in its real dimensions, not the ones Dido had given them, but certainly they could not be faced with mere cynicism. The secret had been unfolded wide-open like an Anatolian flower spreading death through its scent. Everything had been now washed up like a rotten piece of meat on a beautiful shore.*

*Dido got up slowly and with difficulty as if she aged instantly. She was not angry, nor shocked. Her face had a strange peacefulness, as a myriad of thoughts surrounded now her simple mind. They were walking side by side silently. Their moods were completely different. One of them was skeptical and the other relieved. Yet, she was not calm; she waited for her verdict and the waiting slowly rubbed the last traces of patience.*

*How quickly everything changes sometimes! The sky had ceased being clear anymore. A clumsy big spot of clouds made them aware that rain was in the air anytime soon. At the exact moment they entered the T-station. Dido suddenly held her hand. She looked at her with her familiar glance and Calypso's heart was relieved.*

*"-One day you will return!" she told me with a faint smile. She did not convince me though.*

*Sat side-by-side in the metro without their glances meeting, Did said calmly:*

*-Kalypso, I think that you shitted everything completely. You were not faithful either to Michalis or to Alexandra. Was it worth it?*

*-What can I say! A man died because of me.*

*-A lot, I think, she added with austerity.*

*-The relationship with Michalis had been spoiled a long time before Orestes had come into my life. I simply was not able to clear my position with Michalis because I still felt something for him. But he himself never had time nor was he in the mood to sit down and reflect on our situation. And then there appears Orestes. He is extremely enchanting, approachable, he makes me feel like the center of the world, he has time and is willing to spend it with me, to guide me, to help me mature. But he does not want to take a step beyond the discussions. And I lose the measure and I don't know what I want and amidst all this turmoil, Alexandra telling me that she is crazy about him. And I decided to live in silence for a while. Just until the situation clears up. And shit!!!!*

*This is what she said, hiding her face between her hands, and she continued:*

*-And what tortures me most of all is that the kiss that Alexandra witnessed was the farewell kiss. That night after many conversations Orestes had convinced me that the best thing for me would be to go on with my life without him. Because he and I would never be able to be together as a couple.*

CHAPTER 10

# MISTAKES

*How strangely things change sometimes! As if life plays strange games with us to laugh at us. As if constrained in a handicap chair for years, she plays tricks at us through its toothless smile.*

*I learned to drive in London. Reversely. I never understood this particularity of theirs. The sure thing, however, is that it almost cost me my life whenever I attempted to drive in other countries. Theseus taught me how to drive. My mania to keep like crazy whatever card reached my hands led me to Theseus's house one evening. Yes, to the son of Mrs. Sophia whom I had met on the airplane when I first came to London. Necessity sometimes leads you to paths that otherwise you would never have taken. When I took Theseus's personal card that evening I acted intuitively, and I hid it deep down in my pocket without even looking at it. I had absolutely no intention to ever use it, in spite of his good looks.*

*Theseus was the man to whom most of women would be attracted and would like to start a relationship with him. Athletic countenance, kind eyes, handsome hands, wonderful juicy lips, and an air in his walking to the point that without the smallest effort, everyone's eyes unconsciously folded him. Despite his inner strength, he lacked any sense of prowess. He was crystal clear and down to the earth. His feet were deeply rooted in the earth, something that gave his step a nuance of sweet coffee. Thus, he covered the people around him with a pink feeling of security. He belonged to the type of people whose mistakes were so rare as the snowfall in the summer. His life*

*was full of success. At an age when the others are still depend-
ent on their parents, he was independent and successful. The
perfect man, one would think!*

*That perfect man I decided t- meet one evening with an awful
weather, having forgotten how perfect he was! Our meeting
was not exactly the outcome of thought... it was rather one
more game of chance. That Sunday afternoon Dido had dom-
ineered the house because she was newly enamored and was
preparing a surprise for her beloved. For the sake of the surprise, she needed to have the entire house at her disposal. Harry
was for another weekend with his parents, Alexia was at her
girlfriend's house for a project, and I acted like a joker. My
presence would spoil Dido's effort to seduce her red-haired
Irish love. I had to disappear the entire afternoon. Perhaps also
in the evening!*

*-No problem! I said and I disappeared smiling but heavy-heart-
edly. I had no idea where I would spend so many hours, but
I had no choice.*

*She walked for quite some time at the park nearby, she run
out of strength at some point and decided to read a book forgotten in her backpack, but quickly she set it aside due to the
cold that along with the immobility had numbed her hands
and feet. She got up and almost running she arrived at the clos-
est pub. She ordered a glass of red wine and accommodated
herself in front of the window. An awful headache started
piercing her head, her ears buzzed, her nose burnt to the point
that she feared blood would start running from it any moment soon, but she smiled at the idea that shortly she and
Dido covered with the orange fleet cover would drink Jasmin
tea while Dido would narrate all her spicy details to her.*

*Her solitude did not seem that huge in that space. Other women also sat by themselves without seeming to wait for anything to happen or to be stood by someone and enjoyed a small glass of wine, perhaps the last of the week, and were getting ready for a sweet little nap. Observing the people in and outside the pub she spent two entire hours. She had no more strength. Besides, how many hours can one spend with just one glass of wine? For a second glass, there was no word, such a thing was part of the luxuries of old times.*

*She decided to make a phone call home to see how the idyll was progressing. It was not a great idea, but she had no choice. However, after the phone call, she did not have anywhere to go.*

*Suddenly she felt utterly desperate like a rough black seed stuck in her throat. She could not breathe; she became all-red and sweaty in the cold. She was afraid! For the first time in that foreign country, she felt a fear growing within herself so high! A beast ready to cut her down took was swallowing all her breath. It was her punishment. She knew that her luck was to end at some point. The little bell tolls.*

*She wanted badly to be back in Greece! She was taken over by longing without precedent. She walked fast, she cried tacitly and blamed Dido and her Irish jerk. She had made the tour of the block more than five times when she suddenly crashed into a bench. She started searching maniacally for her bag to see if there was any money left, a phone card, whatever could still connect her with the flow of the world. She unearthed whatever pieces of paper she found in her money purse, but desperation went hand in hand with her last hope throwing it away. It soundly crushed it. Weak, she got up, put her bag on her shoulder and started to walk again. Lost! The panic of the first moments had gone away, her tears left her face cold and with her hands deep down in her pockets, she surrendered to her fate. What worse could happen to her than to fall prey to a drunken or a perverse person? Or to have her guts taken out by some drug addicts in their effort to secure their dose by robbing her? She was lost in her thoughts facing a window with very expensive clothing, when she held a piece of paper in her hand. She immediately took it out and read it.*

*It was the personal card of Mrs. Sophia's son! Theseus! His phone number seemed like the number of gold lottery. The look of his as it was becoming clearer in her mind helped her heart to continue to beat. She would call him. At such moments there is no room for shyness. There was no way she would not attempt to give it a try. If only he could be at home! If only, were he alone! If only he could remember her! All these wishes drew the sleigh of her hopes rather far away. When however, the desire is so ardent, perhaps a miracle might happen. It was no time for defeat. She entered a phone cabinet, hung up, dialed up and held her breath. She only has few credit units in her phone card...*

*-Hello!*

*-Hi, Theseus! She tried not to sound overtly desperate.*

*-It's Calypso, I don't know if you remember....*

*-Of course, I remember you! How are you, what's up?*

*-Ah... fine. Hmm... I know it is a little bit surprising, but would you like us to meet?*

*-Great! Only because I am expecting a very important call, would you mind stopping by my house? Where are you right*

*now? If you are somewhere nearby, I could come and pick you up...*

*I was going to faint from my joy. My breath had returned a little bit. Finally, my luck had not completely abandoned me.*

*-If the address on your card is still valid, we are about ten minutes away. You are not far away, I will come.*

*-Do you have a car?*

*-No.*

*-Then you must be crazy! In such a bad weather, I don't allow it. Tell me where you're and I am coming immediately.*

*She did not attempt to play it cool and snobby. She tried to describe in the most detailed way her location, she whispered a "thank you" pouring gratitude and she melted. Acute pain was piercing her skull, she trembled and waited patiently. The ten minutes became twenty and the clear, cold sky down poured a maddened storm in just a few seconds. The stand that was nearby was not enough to keep her dry. When Theseus's car stopped in front of her, she felt as if Christmas were already there. She tried to smile, but she must have looked miserable. Soaked, outside the house for about six hours, penniless and bruised by the cold.*

*-I came late because the phone call I expected took place immediately after we hung down, he apologized.*

*-No problem, I didn't even notice how time flew by, she said, and her clumsy lie burst out like a firework in their eyes.*

*-Sorry! he continued. I was thinking of going somewhere for a drink or for food, but I don't think it is a good idea anymore. It's better to go home urgently. I will cook something. What do*

*you think?*

*What could she say! The only thing she had in her mind was that luckily, he still remembered her and had stopped instead of disappearing. He looked at her and feared she would faint before even hearing her decision. She nodded positively and turned to his side.*

*-Whatever you like, I am a little bit soaked.*

*She had messed up his beautiful car that smelled of coconut and absolute order, but he kept looking at her sweetly. She tried to smile. Instead of this, she burst to tears when their eyes met. He remained speechless. He didn't know what to say. He turned his head and started the engine, sloppily. He turned the radio on and while an English woman in a hysteric voice made a dedication, the uneasiness that had spread all over. Transparent and sharp like glass cut slowly-slowly the last pieces of prowess that were left in her. When they arrived, she had stopped crying. With red and swollen eyes and a nose full of mucus, she tried to stand in front of him in dignity and to justify herself. Something not so easy for someone whom you meet for the first time.*

*-I am sorry for earlier! She spoke. And she continued:*

*-It's nothing, don't pay attention to it. It was simply a bad day, and I am under stress lately.*

*-OK. If at some point you want to talk to me, you will do it, right? If I can be of help...*

*He looked at her with such a steadiness and seriousness that it was a matter of time to open herself to him. Her faint smile became once again an outstretched line.*

*Their first night was somehow unorthodox. He cooked a delicious Greek dish while she ate but a few bites because she had high fever, above 103 F. They did not discuss further details, they only stopped at the day's events. He gave her a dose of fever reliever, she slept on his bed, and he slept on a chair next to her to look after her throughout the night, changing her cold pads. The entire night she was talking in her sleep.*

*-Sorry, I kept saying.*

CHAPTER 11

# SELF-DESTRUCTION

*I often recall the London time. They remember it with a cunning smile. If it could fit in a word, it might be wandering, drinking, clubbing, odd jobs, experiences. A perpetual reality without alarms. My passage lasted almost two years. My professional experiences were many. Bar tender, waitress at Mc Donald's, at high-class restaurants, assistant photographer. Finally, nor could I resist his perfection.*

*I tried almost all the world's flavors as well as a few light drugs. I replaced for quite some time the water with beer, but oddly I retained my flat belly which became a fetish for Theseus, especially when I decided to decorate its navel with a small amethyst, Harry's gift for my good PR I made to our business.*

*With Harry she became best friends, Alexia graduated and returned to the country to distinguish herself, while the motherland did not take much to betray her gloriously. Dido stayed in London where she continued to have an exceptional career. Harry, after the end of his weighty studies in Economics, decided to everyone's surprise to take advantage of the talent he kept secret for so many years. He had a remarkable manual dexterity and an innate inclination to beauty. At first glance, for example, what he felt was the perfect hair color for each type. In the second, if you gave him a chance, he would sit you down in a stool, bench, fence, floor, whatever on earth he could find, and he would transform you. Dido and Alexia were his first clients. Calypso and many other friends then added so that every Saturday morning he was completely booked. Harry also designed her bridal crown. From everything she had on her what had impressed him was her hair.*

*Very quickly, Harry became known in Dido's artistic company, and Alexia's conservative group and thus we were all happy. Initially, the entire enterprise was set up in our house. Dido with me, who I was the lazy of the group, we decorated a room of the house --the lot fell on our own-- and this is how Harry's atelier was born. The ambiance was amazing. We offered various kinds of tea, hot cheese pie from my own hands and whoever wished it, he/she could participate in the procedures. Customers could read books from our rich collection, to flip through sex magazines, help Dido with her monologues, listen to music of their choice, lie down ... Even Greek lessons we would deliver with the haircut, so when they left, besides wonderful heads, you could also see in front of you peaceful human beings with shining eyes, as if they had been reborn. They used to say, "What would I not give for just an hour in Harry's arch!"*

*Harry in six months was almost famous. He could ask for every haircut a small fortune, but he did not do it. The prices were logic and the hordes of people who would arrive at our home outrageous. One of those glorious days, Harry reached 24 hours working without interruption and we who had become friends with the clients at that moment we celebrated in parties. Many of them were having their hair cut on the floor, because during the wait time, they had been crushed!*

*After that night, the big decision was made. The enterprise had to be set up normally and I should move to Theseus's apartment. He did not stand his wife living in a Kibutz, and I had already a huge debt to be able to exercise veto. Harry had accumulated enough money and we had to live like normal people. We found a unified loft, with big curbing windows that served as a storage room in the past and we started our business. The decoration was done in collaboration with some of our clients. Some of them brought personal objects, books, lamps, disks, sofas, pillows and thus with careful placement, the space was transformed into a cozy and humane space, like our house.*

*We printed business cards; we created a website, and we inaugurated the space on a Saturday evening. Dido and Alexia declined politely the job offer along with the generous salary that Harry offered them and thus I remained on my own. His official assistant and muse. Besides, I did not want Theseus to take care of me and my grandma had already stopped her financial support a long time ago!*

*Undoubtedly Harry was talented at hairstyling and I myself in PR. Together with an extraordinary look, the lucky ones gained also psychoanalytical sessions for free. We worked crazy schedules, and we gained crazy money. To our clients list of were also added actors, singers, musicians, radio, and TV producers. During that time, my friends were comprised of famous people rather than common mortals. Dido and Alexia had become pale from their envy. Theseus observed from afar without intervening, at least openly. In the beginning the clients came disguised, but after their first visit, they relaxed, and they felt even better than in their homes. I helped with professional choices, I prohibited divorces, I encouraged the beginning of relationships and all this because I was there, I listened to them, and I made them feel relaxed and protected. Harry's arch produced everyday small miracles.*

*Thanks to their job, they spent two to three extraordinary weekends, guests of their famous friends in their dream houses. One of them especially, quite famous, the first evening offered her a marriage proposal. Theseus had not joined them; he was on a job trip. Fortunately, both of them were heavily drunk and she did not even manage to reply to him. She was nevertheless so attracted to him that along with the confusion that she carried in her head, she ran the next morning to find him and tell him yes. He was sleeping embraced with another guest. To overcome her shock, she run to the beautiful swimming pool that that brimmed on a cliff and dived in. The cold water brought back a relevant equilibrium in her head. It was quite early in the morning, everyone was sleeping. Some were covered by pills and alcohol. Where could she find Harry to tell him about her fiasco?*

*She crossed the huge swimming pool, and she was secretly laughing at her gaffe. She felt beautiful in the water's embrace and not in one's embrace who would smell alcohol. After splashing as much as her stamina permitted her, she went out, covered herself with a soft and perfumed towel jacket and laid down on a recliner gazing at the view far away. She thought of Orestes, Michalis, her parents, Alexandra, Andreas, her home, and she felt a small knot. She thought of her nonexistent future ... Even Theseus was missing from her!*

*However, she was too far from everything! Even the fact that she had quit the University did not fill her with qualms anymore as in the past. Only she could not decide whether she should consider this a failure or the right decision. The many "must" returned her back to her mother's teary face, the boring family feasts, the sad provincial streets, while her many "want" filled her with strength, they launched her to the skies, opened paths to her. If she had followed the "must" she would have never enjoyed that exquisite image that filled her now with such joy!*

*Once again, she had been stuck in the balance of her mind and there was no way for her to receive an answer, when she heard a "good morning." A gentleman with a cup of hot coffee sent the balance far away and brought her thoughts to the present. In an elegant style, he gave her the cup, smiling in assurance. The entire scene reminded her vividly of a publicity and she responded back with a smile. He stood in front of her trying to distract her attention from the wonderful view.*

*-Hi! My name is Maurice, and I am also a friend of these guys. I am perhaps something more. I am their producer!*

*-Nice to meet you! Calypso.*

*-Beautiful name.*

*Thanks.*

*As she was soaked, she felt somehow uncomfortable. He seemed so fresh; he was dressed cozily, and he gave a peaceful calmness. He started drinking in slow gulps and continued to talk.*

*-Beautiful party! Perhaps a little bit more intense than I had in mind, but both of us went to bed early.*

*-Yes, she replied, trying to remember if she had seen him the previous night. I drank a little bit fast, and I unfortunately lost the best part! she replied apologetically.*

*-I don't think you missed something that you are not able to imagine!*

*-Maybe, she replied enigmatically.*

*-Have you ever been to America?*

*-No, I had not had the chance yet.*

*-I think you would like it. I also have my European roots, but*

*I am very lucky that I managed to set my life in such a way that I can stay between New York and Los Angeles, with frequent trips to Europe.*

*-You are lucky and maybe very rich. And you have perhaps set your life in a nice order!*

*My tone was extremely aggressive, and I bit myself, as I was finishing my sentence. What had happened to me? The guy had brought me coffee and was trying to chat with me to spend his time.*

*-Excuse me! I think that my last comment sounded somehow sloppily. It is nice to do what you like and to have found your purpose in life. It is because perhaps I am still having difficulties in this sector!*

*-It is obvious. But you still have some time ahead of you. You will achieve it! Believe in yourself and always be positive. With you and the others. Ah! And don't rush to get married, he teased me as if he knew the gaffe of the previous night.*

*How did he know it? Have there also been other things that have happened that I don't recall? Had he perhaps understood my intention to accept the drunken marriage proposal?*

*The guy was sophisticated! When you are successful, it is fine with you to look at life differently and talk from the position of the powerful. Likewise, when you are not successful, it is also difficult to face objectively everyone who has succeeded in life.*

*Maurice was the epitome of success. An American, born of a French woman artist. Orphan by father at a very early age. A handsome and good person who was lucky to turn his passion into a job! Clever, approachable, willing to help and simple. Permanently enamored with life and women. Hence his three divorces. He laughed that he was the oldest guest, but the only survivor of last night's abuse. He even went jogging because he was a fan of program, and nothing could take him out of the path he had decided for himself.*

*He looked at her and she felt transparent. To a certain degree this behavior of his made her feel relaxed. When you feel that someone knows more than you would ever have the strength to confess, then you lose yourself. You are relaxed. You don't waste your time in unnecessary explanations.*

*This is what she was thinking as an uneasy silence had covered them. But where has this man been last night before consuming two bottles of wine and four martinis? At least she would have talked to someone, she was thinking.*

*He abruptly broke the silence and started talking about himself again. He was talking with pride about all his successful professional moves. He listed an entire list of m sic groups with which he had worked. He said that his secret was his own instinct.*

*-From the first moment I talk with someone, I know exactly what to expect. From the very first notes I will listen to; I know whether a musical piece will become a hit or not. A qualification that most of the time is a blessing, but others it is a curse. The guys, for example, are very good!*

*He also confided in her that if they limit a little bit the use of drugs, they have a lot to offer.*

*She was ready to ask what he was thinking about her, but she was afraid of hearing his answer and thus she remained silent. Nevertheless, he added with a meaningful gesture that her Mediterranean temperament was so obvious that would be impossible not to draw the attention of the Anglo Saxons. Yet this advantage was exactly what would withdraw her aways from the people she was going to be mingling with, he stressed with seriousness. Regardless of if this was the right thing, the assurance in which he was talking to her had started to get on her nerves. In a little while he would be in a position to tell her up to how many tooth fillings she had done, how many lovers she had had and how much money she had in her bank account.*

*After finishing his lecture and updated her on the many wonderful things he had done in his life, he got up to leave. As he was about to leave, he placed a business card on her hand, and he shook it strongly.*

*-If ever your path brings you to our places, don't hesitate to call me. Everyone needs help when found in unknown places.*

*-I will if I find myself in your place. I am sure that I will need help, she said sarcastically.*

*«-I know it! » He replied to her with certainty, and he left.*

*She took his business card smiling, certain that never would she need his help. She did not need any other help! The last time she used a business card, she found herself «bound» hands and feet in a relationship she was unable to cut off. It was time now for her to manage her life by herself. She had to manage everything on her own! She did not owe to anyone anymore. She wanted to stand on her own feet. To decide about herself and not to report to anyone. Not to be in need to apologize and make any concessions.*

*America was not in her immediate plans. Nostalgia had started ringing the first bells. She wanted to return home and make a new start. In her own terms. In her mind there was not the audacity of wandering anymore. Especially after last night night's party, the throwing, the coituses, the coke that was at every place she would throw a glance, the «innocent» smoking, she felt that her inhibitions and her stamina very soon would abandon her. Besides she would not see any reason to keep her mind clear and her soul immaculate. The people around her did not differ from her at all. They were neither better nor worse. Only they were doing something that offered them fulfillment, they had money, glory, houses, love, even if every night changed face with some coke in their nares.*

*Her own nares were clean, her pockets empty, and her mind stuck in memories. Emotionally empty like a step, with the nails of death hanging from her spine permanently. She could not fit in with any plan. She suffocated in her solitude; she did not stand the crowd. She wanted to end her relationship with Theseus, but she did not have the guts to stay alone. She felt that she could do everything and yes, she did nothing.*

*If only she could escape from this house, but how since it was built on a rock?*

*-I must go to make it to my flight, Maurice said. It's a pity that our friends are still sleeping. Tell them to communicate with me as soon as possible. Nice meeting you! I hope we will talk soon.*

*-Bon voyage!*

*I was certain that we would never talk again.*

*As he was becoming more and more distant, she thought that his hair would be better on him if it had a tiny darker shade. She had taken this weird thing from Harry. She threw a quick glance at the business card and went to find her phone directory. She kept it along with the other cards and perused indifferently her directory looking at the phone numbers of her latest acquaintances. Her eye fell on Michalis' phone number. She had kept his business card as a souvenir and in the back pocket a picture of him. She did not take it out of her place. Where could he be? she wondered. Not that she had any intention of attempting to find him.*

*«-Don't come to my life again», he had told me when he left. Very harsh words, indeed, especially since it was the last thing, I remember hearing from his lips.*

*She dressed and went back to her favorite place. Her good mood had disappeared. As Maurice did. They could have fine conversations, she thought. He seemed cultivated, polite, and direct. A little bit arrogant, as well! But no one is perfect.*

*-How stupid I am! She said out loud.*

*She should have asked him to take her with him to London. From this desert it was impossible to escape now by herself. And today she could not stand any further alcohol or partying. It's such a beautiful day today! Will the others ever manage to enjoy it, or will they wake up with the first nigh light?*

*Her "almost" husband woke up. He approaches her and kisses her on her front. He asks her if she slept well. She tells him that she met Maurice who expects their news as soon as possible. He discloses to her that the entire night Maurice had his eyes fixed on her.*

*-Who had his eyes fixed on me? Maurice? When? I don't recall having met him last night, she says with eyes wide open by surprise. She learns with delay that Maurice arrived when*

*she had already been overdrunk and had gone up on the table singing Greek songs. After her little show she slept almost on the chair and he took her and accommodated her on a bed, because everyone else was "busy".*

*She felt shame. She was all night long next to an unknown man who offered to look after her. I only hope I did not throw up, nor did I snore or talk while sleeping, she whispered.*

*-He didn't tell me anything like that, he faintly tells her, and she thinks to herself that this explains Maurice's behavior. Finally, he is not such a jerk! Rather I am very stupid!*

*-He is a very fine guy! Adds her friend and she feels worse than before. Come on, little stupid you, don't look at me like that! He did not rape you! He was tired, you were drunk, and the beds were not enough for all of us. Simply he laid next to you! I know you would rather sleep with me, but somebody else had priority. Today, however, I am free, he said and went for a dive.*

*-Sure, stupid you! She said with a smile in impeccable Greek.*

*When at long last Harry woke up, her anger had somehow been gone away. She narrated her story to him with one breath and waited for his reaction.*

*-I don't think you are right regarding the color of his hair. He rather needs some silver highlights on his temples.*

*-Holy shit! Is that you only have to say? Is it because your mind is full of "snow" and the only thing you see is hair? If it were you to fall prey at the hands of an unknown person, I would never let you in the hands of an unknown!*

*He shook himself as if he was hit by electricity. Unjust though!*

*-You are right, sweetie! I have no idea what has taken me lately. Do you know though that I am not a jerk and that I am concerned about you? And, if you want to know, it was only a little bit more alcohol!*

*-I know, but as a matter of fact you abandoned me for a fuck. Was it at least worth it?*

*-Now you are becoming tough. I asked for your pardon. What else should I do?*

*-To show your pardon to me in deeds, not in words! She said and got up.*

*At some point she ought to talk to him the hard way. He had been donned the cloak of arrogance and was degrading himself in steady steps. If he continued like this, his star would shine away quickly. She went for a walk in the garden around the house and when she returned everyone had already woken up. And they had already started the first drinks. She did not feel well. Chills stripped her body, and the smell of the alcohol suffocated her. Harry approached her and told her that he had found a lift for them to depart.*

*-I can't, she replied. I don't feel well.*

*-You are a little pale, like a ghost, he said, touching her front and taking her by her hand. They went up to a big room. He laid her down on the bed and called the host. Soon, he returned with a maiden, a soup, and a thermometer. She threw up, had chills, diarrhea, and fever.*

*Food poisoning!*

*-Fuck my bad luck! She screamed once they left shutting the door behind them.*

*Harry and several of the guests suffered from the same symptoms. Others were throwing up and others kept partying all night long. At some point, everyone was quiet. The first daylight arrived. She felt better and wanted to leave as soon as possible. She felt like a hostage in that house. Theseus had not called at all. He was angry with her because he did not want to let her come alone here. When he would learn about her shameful behavior, he would take his revenge.*

*With the exception of her bad moments, that two-day retreat was going to become a landmark in Harry's career. And to her own life, for other reasons. Somewhere in the vertigo, the flirts and her own throwing ups, Harry conceived a crazy idea. He took his tools and started doing pudenda hair styling instead of head hair styling. No female guest left without Harry's cut.*

*Thus, that night the most famous pudenda hair stylist was born. All this news about what had happened in that villa that night was soon spread everywhere and the following week he kept booking appointments. Famous and ordinary women stood in the queue and paid a lot of money to have their pudenda get Harry's signature. And he in his turn, managed to satisfy the craziest idea in color and shape.*

*Banana, strawberry, St. valentine's heart, dollar sign for the forthcoming IPO, Chanel, or Gucci for the Paris Fashion Show, YES for the pending marriage proposal. Whatever one could imagine! A pudendum combed by Harry had the potential to become a passport for a successful marriage or a ticket to the fashion world, of Hollywood, the music arena even of the science world.*

*If your pudenda had the right hairstyle, you could walk with your head upwards!*

CHAPTER 12

# BROKEN

*The world did not change all of a sudden. Simply our own friendships were somehow eccentric and experienced that change a little bit more intensely. People at that time were hysterical and panic stricken. It is not that easy to come to terms with the idea that one day you may die of suffocation due to a stupid chemical that someone has thrown on your train wagon or when someone with a machine gun targets you while you are calmly sitting and drinking a glass of wine in the name of a stupid religion.*

*Likewise, it is so easy to accept the probability of watching your savings from many years of hard work and good budgeting disappear, as the bourses of the world are collapsing. Likewise, it is not easy to swallow the image of your proud country to disappear in front of your eyes, shameful! You are unable to believe how your parents, your uncles, your teachers, and their entire generation have imprisoned you in a country without a future.*

*With how many bombs is it possible for someone to clean up the messiness and corruption of so many years?*

*Such bright ideas were hidden in the minds of people during those years when they would take their children to school, when they would go shopping or they would go out for entertainment. Everywhere there was a fog of fear, even when everyone pretended that the situation was under control.*

*But it is not possible for someone to hide forever from life. Life is beautiful and you want to live it. It is important for someone to feel that there is a future ahead, a possibility and preconditions for things to be improved; that better days are ahead if you work hard! That whatever span of life you are destined to live, you will be in a position to taste it with dignity. Thus, as all were overwhelmed by maddened terror, they started going out and living more dangerously than before, especially to exorcise terror. It has perhaps to do with the fact that when you face death upfront, it ceases to scare you anymore. It seems like you have thrown yourself in the black ski base and there is no point of return but the decent. You will gaze at the hill with awe; you will take a deep breath and you will get started. At the first descents, your feet will tremble, but you will stay straight. You will be happy with your success, you will feel strong, almost invincible and amidst vertigo, you will forget fear. You will speed up and in the best scenario you will end up in the hands of a lifesaving team. In the worst-case scenario, you may crush on a tree. There is, of course, also the possibility for you to succeed, but it is so tiny! In any case, what you will always remember will be the moment when you defeated fear. For such a moment perhaps, an entire life might be worthy... Perhaps!*

*People wanted to live without terror. They used to go out, to drink, to dance, to make love. Whatever they did, they did it intensely and passionately. Until last fall! Everything in the beginning seemed beautiful, vivid, healthy. People abandoned fear, pain, lies, disappointments, qualms and everything flew by beautifully without wounds. Only open minds were everywhere; able to emerge out of the fogs that suffocated their entire life; ready to become free and fly high above the conventional, the commonplace, the boring! One had the sense that the entire society had been transformed into something su-*

*perior, indeed civilized, and thus there was no need for feeling rooted somewhere; that one could live independently and yet be able at every moment whenever needed to find a mother's hug, a lover, a child protector, a wise man, a piece of advice.*

*The change that everyone was seeking like crazy, never came. Perhaps because it was sought in madness and thus it crashed under their feet in their panic. And then they passed on the other side. Before even being able to mourn the happiness that was tacitly dying out underneath their bloody feet, they harmed each other and destroyed each other not by a chemical as everyone was fearing of, but by greed. The thousands of children that were born during that insane time, had all of them in their glance the arch as the last remainder of the civilized society that dared to exist for a short time. But all of them, twenty years after that fatal night, donned their body with myriads of explosives and sunk the world into darkness forever. Even those kids who were born in the "dark" needed hope to be able to live.*

*Thousands of naked babies with genitalia of an adult chased me one of the many nights during which I had drunk a cocktail of light drugs and I had been sunken in my hallucinations. It was the pretext for me to pass through a glass, to spend a month in the hospital in complete immobility and with shattering fractures and the beginning of a new life. Theseus once again salvaged me, took care of me and drafted even Mrs. Sophia for extra care towards me and cut me off from Harry, who after six months ended up in jail for drugs use, fraud, harassment... I never learned the truth! I found him many years later when he became famous again! Some people are born lucky, and Harry was one of them.*

*In any case, the basic thing during that period of my life was that Theseus committed to putting order in both my life and his life. I had passed through an entire glass in the hope to cut the thread of my life while he made the goal of his life to find those edges of the threads and form tight knots. In his plans our lives had a common target, regardless of the fact that I had not been asked about this. Besides, during that time my contact with reality was not that good to be able to express my opinion on any matter. He was the one who made the decision and planned the action plan. Before even my recovery after the accident, he loaded me with his mother on a plane and I found myself in Athens, in his parents' house, preparing for my university exam period. He had taken care of everything! All my books were in his room, the professors were aware of my situation or rather of my decline, and thus the only thing that was missing was my own good mood.*

*It was nice that I was again in Greece. Although things had radically changed. I was able to breathe again freely far from Theseus. I had a beautiful house where I lived, two people standing by me at every moment, I did not have a penny, but I didn't care at all –because money was limited for everyone at that time—and above all I had won in a strange way, the exclusive interest of a wonderful man. I had all the mistakes one can commit in a relationship and Theseus kept forgiving me. Why?*

*She did not find any value at all in the diploma she was trying to get, but the effort was worthy, if only for Theseus's sake. She needed to try harder than she had initially imagined, because she had lost every contact with the subject matter. For six months then she was an exemplary student. Either because she felt obliged to Theseus's wonderful parents --and here one wonders which argument he had used to convince them to accept me--, her pride of honor that Theseus systematically kept it high, she finally graduated.*

*During her stay in Athens, she did not communicate with anyone, Euro. Theseus came several times to visit her, and they communicated on a daily basis. He kept asking her whether she had a good time and if she was missing anything. During those months she didn't miss anything. Only her freedom!*

*When she finally got her degree, Theseus gave her an expensive watch as a present to acquire a better sense of time from now on, he told her with a smile. She did not call her parents even for the graduation ceremony. She had no one from her relatives to call. Her grandma had died. She did not go to her funeral; went however to her grave and lit a candle in her memory and laid on the marble and cried under the alert glance of Theseus's mom. She whispered to her ear that soon she would go visit her.*

*I was in the packed hall, beautifully dressed in my new watch, Theseus, and his parents. In the overall joyful situation, I was the only one who was crying. Mrs. Sophia thought it was because I was moved that I managed to succeed after so much effort I put into this. Theseus thought that I felt I was in a difficult position because the watch was very expensive. They kept hugging me and continued their own conversations while I was mourning my lost personality. I was mourning the lost path that I was not even in a position to engrave.*

*The next day they left on vacation. She had no idea where they were going. Theseus had organized everything. As always! He had taken care of everything. He even had bought her a bathing suit! She should have been happy and careless, but she was thinking how unlucky she was that she did not die when they passed through the glass window. She felt some-thing equivalent to the fourth baggage. She had made so many efforts to escape those who oppressed her and yet she had let herself without any battle to enter a most hated situation. Amidst all this, she realized that the only feeling she ever had for Theseus was gratitude. Yet this feeling by itself was not enough to sustain a love relationship.*

*He, on the other hand, absolutely devoted to his plan, celebrated his victory. He did not see, or he did not want to see her indifference. His planning, once again, was successful. Their first evening in Santorini, he announced to her that after their vacations they would go to London to search for a new home, that he had been promoted and thus earned almost a double wage and therefore there wouldn't be any problem at all for the next step.*

*"-Which next step?" she whispered.*

*"-To get married, of course!" he replied to her.*

*"-I don't think I am ready for such a thing", she dared to say.*

*"-Of course, you are!" he told her. "Perhaps you have not understood in what situation you are involved."*

*"-What do you mean?" she asked. She did not get any answer. He looked at her enigmatically, but she did not dare to think what he could possibly mean.*

*He continued as if he had not listened to her, telling her that his parents had agreed with his decision, but especially hi himself was very proud that she had been able to get through all this turmoil so successfully. He told her that he was not shameful of her anymore, because he knew that she is good by heart and thus she would be able to stand next to him in the future in dignity. He announced to her simply the continuation of his plan that he had in his mind. He did not look at her eyes even for a moment.*

*Inside herself she felt ready to explode but she seemed calm, sweet, and silent. She had surrendered. As if she was watching a movie with the story of an unfortunate woman who lacked the courage to vindicate her own life. She was looking first at him and then at the watch on her wrist that artfully covered the traces of the glass fragments, and she felt that it had already become a noose in her neck. After many bottles of wine, they found themselves in the room. Lying on the beautiful sky-looking bed, they started kissing. It was the first sign of tenderness of the entire evening. Their kiss looked rather like a friendly hug. She did not wish to be there. She did not want him to touch her.*

*Even if she had missed the warmth of the hands in love!*

*Until that night, Theseus was always very tender. I told him that I felt dizziness and I did not want to continue. He did not reply to me. When he tied my hands back tightly on my shoulder, I realized that it was not an erotic game. His look was different. I had in front of me an unknown man. I reacted and I told him that I was not in the mood for games. He stuck his shirt in my mouth, and he told me that after what he had done for me, he had every right to do whatever he wished with me. He did everything possible to make me feel degraded. Under his full control. For two consecutive nights he kept me imprisoned in that room. One evening he dragged me almost insensitive to the airport and we returned to London. My entire body was wounded. People were looking at me with pity and he was describing to them my fake accident. I begged him endless times to let me go and endless times to kill me.*

*"-You are my trophy wife for years to come!" He kept answering me smiling. "-You must get used to this. This is only some erotic games!"*

*She thought that everything was a strange, horrible joke. Her confused mind was trying to understand why. The first night after the return she suffered uninterrupted bleeding. He abandoned her in front of a hospital and disappeared.*

CHAPTER 13

# LIFE RE-INVENTED

*Fortunately, Dido was still in London. She was notified by the hospital and came immediately to see me. She was informed about my situation, and she was very careful with me. I did not tell her who was responsible, she insisted on hearing from my lips the name of Theseus and argued that I ought to take him to court. I wanted to disappear and forget everything that had happened. I feared that he would come back and would find me. I had the feeling that he was already overseeing my movements. Dido moved quickly and carefully and once I got out of the hospital, I left for America. The same evening! Together with my friends who had formed the music group. Music kept playing an important role in my life. This time it saved me. Fortunately, my friends were doing well at that time, and they had arranged for a tour in America.*

*All of them had been informed about my adventure and tried to help me in any way they could. After what had happened to me, I was negative and suspicious. Unfortunately, not the best company I could have. They brought me with them halfway through their tour until Maurice intervened. He was the one who found me a job and a house. A tiny room in the basement of a villa and a job that barely permitted me to cover my basic expenses. But I felt good, and I had hope to restart my life. I did not make plans for my future, I simply let the days fly by, just like Sisyphus. Time flew by and I did not have the luxury to remain insensitive. I was alive and I ought to behave analogously. No matter how I looked at my life as a huge void. I don't remember much from that period of my life. I don't know how I was, how I behaved, how I worked, how I survived.*

*I know, however, that there also exist good people in the world. People who stood by me and I was not even able to thank them.*

*I used to live on the hills of Los Angeles, and I was going back and forth to my work by bike. I would Maurice only during our company's weekly meetings. He was like a king in a beautiful kingdom full of accolades who admired him and begged for a glance of his, praise from him. We would not exchange but two-three chats a week. There would be periods when I would not see him for months. After five years, he invited me to his office to announce to me, along with the them boss of mine, my promotion. It was not a promotion that would secure me an upgrade to a skyscraper and the markets in Rodeo Drive, but it was my first personal victory. That day, he invited me to go out for dinner. It was the first time we would talk about something different from work.*

*These five years I was working like crazy. Most of the days of the week I was sleeping at my office pretending I needed to complete last-minute chores, but the real reason was that I was afraid of staying home alone, even though I continued living in the small basement of a house surrounded always by people and chats. As far as my landlords who were Maurice's friends, I met them just a few times and in the entire span I stayed at their home we barely exchanged a few chats.*

*Yet after my promotion I needed to collaborate with Maurice on a different level. Finally, after five slow years, Maurice entrusted me a seminal position and by no means I wanted to disappoint him.*

*I did not know unfortunately that responsible for my new position was not Maurice but my former boss who had no idea about my accomplishments up to that moment, not to mention what else I would be able to accomplish in the future. I was in charge of new artists, full of flame, passion, and dreams. Every day I became acquainted with something new. Their passion and their steady faith in their work and their talent kept me always alert. As if I gained a share of shine from their own success! I was the first obstacle they had to overcome, but perhaps also their most ardent supporter throughout the entire process. It was proved that I had a good instinct and that I had a good ear for everyone. The big truth nevertheless was that I was not in a mood anymore to talk and thus I overcame my vanity, acquiring a genuine interest in the lives and ideas of others.*

*All these years there was between us an invisible electric wire that we carefully avoided touching. When he decided to invite me for dinner, perhaps his instinct showed him that it was the appropriate moment to push that button. Always there was between us something exceptional. On my behalf, there was an immense admiration and appreciation for the second chance he so generously had offered me. On his behalf, I had no idea how he looked at me. I had decided that there was no room in my heart for any man anymore. Because of them my life up to that moment had been shattered many times. I did not feel any need to be with someone, I did not feel any sexual desire. To be precise, this matter was absent from my mind. It was as if I lived a second childhood, when you don't know anything about love, when you are not interested in learning about it and when certainly you are not interested in participating in it. I belonged to a neutral sex.*

*I lived out of chance and because I happened to be a strong human being. Rather the opposite. A psychoanalyst might have been helpful in figuring this out, but I decided to reconcile* with myself in my own pace and by saving my money and my emotions. Besides, I was afraid that in order to analyze whatever I had lived up to that moment, I would have to spend the remainder of my life in psychoanalytic sessions. Moreover, I would have to recall and narrate all the torturing details that I was trying to forget in every possible way.

I decided to go out for dinner with Maurice without further complicating the invitation. To him I could easily speak about everything. Besides, he already knew most of the events of my adventurous past life. Thus, we began on a new basis. Most of our discussion concerned our work. Yet, there were also moments when we also talked about himself, his daughter, his divorces, his ex-wives, and his present lovers. His life was undoubtedly interesting and the way he described it very inventive and entertaining. He gave the impression that he was grateful to his Fate for everything he had experienced, both good and bad, beautiful, and ugly. I on my part had not done my own transgression. I was listening to him, and I was thinking that one day I may be able to see life the way he sees it. Not so seriously, not so dramatically, not so absolutely! I felt lucky however that I could forget my own life in the torpor of the events of his own life. Besides, my life had a problematic present that was based on a problematic past that I wanted to forget. The future preoccupied me only to the extent that it was related to my job. I wanted to succeed because I wished fulfilment only through my own eyes. Apparently, I had not completely overcome my childhood syndrome. I wanted to succeed in making him feel proud of me. I had made one more right choice if only out of compassion!

Nevertheless, it was quite tiresome to always try to do my best, to make my transgression. He did not need my own success *in order to feel successful. He had a thousand things in his mind and surely, he was not interested in covering my own insecurities through my own productivity. There were moments when he was not even aware of my preoccupations. It took me a long time to realize that he didn't give a damn about my own intervention. But in my own childish gullibility, I believed he had eyes everywhere!*

*The traps of the mind play strange tricks on you. They fill you with wounds that you notice always last. The people around you see them, talk to you about them, trying to awaken you. But you, like a long-extinguished volcano, do not react, not even to the few outbursts of smoke. Sleeping beauty, yet at the same time so tragic, you are lost in a sleep so gray that looks like a white step. You are sunken in an endless laguna similar to a scenery of hallucinatory visions hoping to see the blue and humane mermaid of the fairy tales to give you the kiss of life. But mermaids are not real even though you continue seeking them during the dizzy evenings, when nothing is in its place and when time is irrelevant because you are not in apposition to notice it and the pleasure that you so much need comes faintly like an outcome of a process that has nothing to do with the erotic touch that you miss so much.*

*The word traps keep chasing you, abasing you, disorienting you. Only a word. A word, in dexterous hands, becomes a bow-tie, a knot, a noose, even a star. Only a word, uttered by different tiny lips sounds in the empty rooms of the mind like praise or an insult. Only a word, naked of feelings, traces an itinerary. Donned in colors of war may be capable of changing course. Target!*

*I had already completed some thirty-odd years of life and...*

*what had I achieved? I had arrived at the edge of the earth trying to find my personal freedom, balance, and security. I saw different things, the lives, and souls of people that I had never imagined, I experienced pain, humiliation, vanity, success, fear, arrogance, love, contribution, death. Intensely. But still I was not able to understand what happiness is if there is somewhere and how one can reach it if she wishes it.*

*I adored the sun. I work now only with the shutters closed not to see the daylight. The beauty! For it is so easy for someone to get lost and then the thoughts of the heart begin. But I drowned my heart that first night in Santorini. And since then, it never returns but only in my dreams. Then we are both harmless. And silent! I sleep only four hours a day. When I sleep at the office, I sleep a little bit more, because I fear less. I ran. I ran a lot. I run in forests, mountains, parks, beaches. Whenever I have spare time, I run. Immobility gives birth to unwanted thoughts. I ran not to think. I try to escape my Furies. I think only of my job. I don't leave any room to myself. I want to succeed. Only in that way I believe I will love myself again. Only in this way I believe that I will gain others' respect. Especially Maurice's respect.*

*I smoke and I drink a lot. Otherwise, my sleep is light and brings dreams with the odor of rottenness and blood. I eat very little, and my silhouette reminds rather of a teenager, although my face shows its age. For around my eyes there exist creeks of memory, lost dreams and sickened loves. My eyelashes do not play with the sunlight, as they used to do, when they looked like velvet wings of a butterfly, but they rather look like tint muddy digs of tears of the past. I don't smile anymore, and I talk little. Maurice immediately understood all this when we went for dinner that night. After five years. Until then he had* not even noticed it. He did not attempt to lecture me. I appreciated it enormously. I am not in the mood to change anything. I don't care when I will die. I will not be sorry for anything, and no one will be sorry for me.

-As a matter of fact, tell me, do you like America? Wasn't I right?

-Yes. It is beautiful, at least here. I am ready to say more, but it doesn't matter. Let the discussion flow without drama.

-I haven't asked you for a long time, but I imagine you have already adjusted. And I am sure that everything at work goes well. This is why we are here today, to celebrate your promotion!

-Five years have already passed, I whisper, and therefore I have already found my routine. And yes, at work, everything is wonderful. And I thank you! I did not have the chance to thank you in person. Without your intervention back then, I don't know what the end would have been.

-I am sure that you too would do the same had you bee in the same position. Five years is indeed a long time, I had not realized it. My second marriage lasted barely three!

This is what he said to her laughing and invited the waiter with a gesture. He talked to him in a charming and familiar tone, as if he were there every night.

-I want to impress our sweet Calypso tonight, because she is the guest of honor.

-We will do our best to make this night unique! The waiter replied returning the familiar courtesy.

Indeed, that evening was unique. She allowed herself to think *that there also exist good people. People who will behave well towards her without expecting anything in return.*

*Of course, no one is perfect. Certainly not myself, neither himself of course. We became drunk that night. I drank so much that I unlocked my heart on my own. And as if this were not enough, I also lost the key!*

*I slept at his house that night. In the absolute darkness, I slept in his lap for ten entire hours. Without interruption in his lap for ten entire hours. Without interruption, without nightmares. I was not able to go to work the next day. For by no means, I wanted to leave him. I had missed the body touch so much! We played true then both of us from work and we spent the day at home, cooking, talking, listening to music, drinking. We walked to the beach hugged and we played with the waves like children.*

*We danced at the sound of a distant music, and we laughed with our hearts without even the help of alcohol. We made love at noon on the verandah, and everything came with absolute naturalness. We found our rhythm without trying hard.*

*It was extremely difficult for me to calm down and enjoy this new situation. The lessons of the past had made me very cautious. I tried hard to be appeased. I was struggling. I did not want any sad memory to get in the way and spoil my day. I did not want my mind to start the comparisons and look for inexistent signs. I freed my mind from high expectations. I only lived for the day. And it was wonderful! And I didn't care if there would be other days. I only knew that I could not stand the exile to which I had subsumed myself anymore. I had paid enough if I had to pay for anything.*

*Maurice had a wonderful music collection, as was expected of course. He had playlists according to mood, age, month, emotion, food, whatever a man's mind could possibly imagine. He matched music with any circumstances, as others chose the right wine for the food. At his home he was almost a different person, much more relaxed, funnier. He wandered barefoot with a glass in his hand and asked me the toughest questions with an almost childish innocence.*

*After he first made his de profundis confession, I talked to him about Orestes who had died, about Michalis who had abandoned me, about Theseus who had raped me and whereas I was cursing love and men, in between tears and laughing, I told him that whatever I did all these years, I did it for him. To pay off for the big favor he rendered me. For the second chance he offered me. And as I almost cried out my last words, I froze. And I was clueless. He too along with me. And I started a series of failed attempts to change the subject to appease the ambiance. But it was late. I had already confessed that all this time I begged for a glance of his. I told him smiling, that had I left with him that day when I met him, I would have been saved from Theseus. He smiled, came next to me and he kissed my hand softly.*

*"-You saved yourself! Don't forget it."*

*I could not remember when it was the last time, I had received such a tender, warm kiss. With that kiss I think I started living again. I started to inhale deeply. I had again a purpose in my life. To live!*

*I was happy and his good mood made all ghosts of the past faint little by little. I felt I was finally able to escape them. My feet started again becoming strong and I was ready to confront them.*

*I had tried hard to live far from everyone and now for the first time I felt that I did not want to be lost for everyone on this distant continent. I remembered swiftly my mother, my sister, my father, my grandma and inside me their awakened flames ready to melt their frozen images. My grandma and my father had died. The only thing I could do for them was to search in my mind for whatever beautiful they had given me. No anger existed within me anymore. Each one of us had paid for his own mistakes. It was of no importance anymore who was more responsible.*

*Maurice talked only about two women: his mother and his daughter. The one represented strength and inspiration and the other the compass, the Polar star. Their presence and absence equally intense.*

*With Maurice she started going out now as a couple and after six months they decided to live together. Two years later Calypso got a non-remunerated leave of absence because they decided that it was time for her to write her first book, something she wanted very much. However, things did not evolve the way they had planned it.*

*The many trips somehow disoriented me. We used to spend our time very beautifully and this feeling was something entirely new for me. I enjoyed every single moment and I decided to delay a little bit my effort to become an author. I stopped running like crazy and I started doing yoga. I paid attention to our nutrition; I started sleeping normally and breathing normally. The days I was walking on a tight rope had ended. After so many years of absolute solitude I longed to be among people, to share beautiful experiences, to talk, to laugh, to have fun and to have a normal relation with a man who loved me and showed it at every minute.*

*I was happy and enamored! I was even ready to return home to see my mother, my sister, my aunts, my uncles, my cousins, my old classmates... Michalis... Where could he be indeed? Was he happy? Had he gotten married, had he had children? Has he ever thought of me? Questions of desperation of fainted loves! He was the one who went abroad first, and I almost stayed there. Strangely things turn out in life's path. You let yourself for a little bit in her torpor and you wake up in places in which you never expected to be, or you remain in the same places, where you were certain that you would never inhabit. I don't know which of the two should cause more fear!*

*The years I lived with Maurice in America looked like a movie. Something like Great Gatsby! Grandiose parties, beautiful and interesting people, sweet excess. Exquisite houses, outstanding landscapes, congenial creations. Both of us were trying to erase the past. Whatever we had lost in the past we were trying to substitute for it through excess. Two people passionate about life and with each other. But as always happens in movies, time flows with the speed of the screen writer, without necessarily the existence of a logic coherence. Thus, the first five years of our joint life ran and flew by leaving me many wonderful memories. Every day was like a celebration, a party. There was no sense of routine in my daily life, only surprises. Yet, this was not the case for Maurice's life. For him all this was part of a daily routine which he was trying to live differently in order to manage to see it again through my own eyes. However, all this actually happens only in real movies.*

*At some point I managed to finally finish my first book! It was published the fifth year of our joint life and along with it the first clouds in our relationship appeared. The change came indeed out of the sky. As I was tasting the first taste of success of my book, Maurice's daughter was killed in a airplane crash. The moment I was ready to begin my tour, he collapsed and was never able to overcome his loss. He withdrew in himself and in his office, he developed phobias about life, death, love, sleep, food. He refused to sleep out of fear not to die and at the same time he also refused to eat and to at least drink water, in order to die. He did not want to travel anymore because all media of transportation caused claustrophobia in him. He suffered from panic crises, and therefore I had to travel. He did not want us to make love because he himself felt that he did not have the right in joy while his child had been killed. He stopped working because he believed that his child's death occurred due to some superior force to punish him for his arrogance! He begged me to leave his life because he loved me very much and he did not want to destroy me. He was right, but I was not ready to abandon him. Perhaps because I was unable to understand the extent of the problem. I was sure that my love and my care would help him recover.*

*The doctors were that certain though. In the beginning they were reassuring, but when this situation lasted more than two months, they decided that he needed urgent care because his health had been tremendously weakened and my sole love and care was not enough. He was hospitalized and I returned to the real world. To the bills, the contracts, the insurances, attorneys. I felt ready to face all these duties, but Maurice's situation made me very skeptical! For so many years I had been well accommodated under his shadow! I need not repeat the mistakes of the past. Once again, I used crutches. Shame on me of course, but it was a little bit late to apologize. Besides he was not able to show generosity! Sometimes I felt that he almost hated me. Perhaps he also considered me responsible for his daughter's death.*

*I was trying to rehabilitate and adjust to reality and make my priority. Never before had it occurred to me that Maurice might never recover. The insecurities that for many years I tried to get rid of started suffocating me again. Should I confront reality on my own? It was a probability that I allowed myself to think of it only once per day. Certainly, many times it remained the only thought of the day.*

*My publisher asked for new material, and I could not fill even a page. It was impossible to continue my effort to become an author. I had not even a trace of inspiration anymore. Whatever I started, ended up being a pitiful repetition of the effort of the previous day. Without his support, my mind seemed as if not working anymore. I was afraid.*

*In the meantime, time passed, and his health condition did not show any improvement. And at the moment I was ready to accept it, I became pregnant. A visit to the clinic was accompanied by intercourse. When I discovered it, I did not know whether I should cry or laugh. Amidst the entire insanity of the situation this thing also occurred. Could I disclose it to him? Should I, do it? Given his health condition I also wondered whether I should keep it or not. After a series of meetings with the doctors and special preparation I found the strength to reveal my pregnancy to him. The specialists judged it was then the right moment for me to tell him about it. And indeed, they were right. From the moment he heard the news his health condition improved day by day. We arrived at the point that perhaps we should consider the case of his return home.*

*He finally returned home during Christmas of that year, after almost a year in the clinic. Due to his long hospitalization, our financial situation could be barely characterized bearable. The party I organized for his return home took place thanks to the generosity of our few friends. That evening I had thought that all the bad things had gone. He looked so healthy, smiling, ready to restart his life afresh. He even looked younger and stronger than before! And he was so happy that he had forgotten the reason for which we had thrown that party. He hugged me, he kissed me all night long and was teasing himself about the age at which he would become again a father. In two months, he would become 54 years old and for the second time father. The fact of the second time had been carefully not mentioned. Even he behaved as if it would be the first time for him to become a father.*

*The next day he began his schedule as exactly he used to do in the past. The first thing he did after his return was a playlist with lullabies for the baby. Now he worked in a more intense pace to make up for the lost time, as he used to say. The doctors had advised him to start with a more relaxing daily program, but he thought that there was no reason for him to postpone anything. I for my part took it as a good sign that he wished to return the sooner to the work that he so much liked. He was away from me for many hours, but he was tender and protective when he was with me—rarely though—and thus I could not ask for more. Besides I was very careful in this regard.*

*After much effort, I was able to behave towards him normally, avoiding burdening him with worries, problems, grouching and especially demands.*

*-I don't want you to worry about anything. I am fine! I feel great! I function with greater clarity and my energy is almost unextinguished. You should concentrate on your books. Everything will be fine!*

*-I am glad to hear this, I thought to myself, and I wondered where truth ended and where falsehood began.*

*-I need to catch up with many things and I must hurry up. I will need to schedule several trips. If you wish, you can come with me, but it would be better for you to get some rest and concentrate on your own things.*

*I had no reason not to believe him and I wanted to believe that he had overcome all his turmoil. The trips started again. For me they were severely forbidden. Again, I started spending endless hours of solitude and stress. Maurice by now was functioning differently. Even his way of working had changed. He seemed as if he was experimenting, as if he sought to try out his own limits. He followed new diets, he read books on new religions, tried alternative medicine. He started visiting places with positive energy, Ojai, California, Sedona, Arizona, in order to balance his inner beats.*

*I was not close enough to him most of the time-mainly because I was not in agreement with all these approaches and their whatever outcomes- and because to a great extent he did not give me permission. Thus, it was impossible for me to locate him. He did not answer my phone calls, I left him endless messages to which he never listened. I felt that his colleagues were trying to disorient me or to scare me. Sometimes I was certain that they were trying to cover him up. I know that during the last two months of my pregnancy he had occasional sex with other women because there must have been no more than two times in total that we had made love from the moment he learned about my pregnancy. These last months I felt rather like a friend who stayed at his home than his companion.*

*I could not stand the idea that I had to start anew. With also a kid this time, I was terrified. I was not ready to proceed without fighting. I tried to talk to him many times. Sometimes I would find the man I loved but some other times not.*

*-Maurice, I understand that you went through a very bad period, but I am here for you. Tell me how I can help you.*

*-I feel great! Why do you say this? It's been years that I haven't felt so creative, he kept telling me hugging me tightly.*

*-Maybe it's the inspiration drawn from our little miracle, he added and kissed my belly.*

*All these happened during the good days.*

*-Maurice, I am trying to communicate with you lately and you are not answering my calls. Where are you?*

*-I am fine! I was lost in my thoughts, sweetie…*

*-I am waiting for you to return two days now and the only thing you have to say is that you were lost in your thoughts…*

*-Yes, Calypso. I was lost in my thoughts, and I was in a mood to do something different.*

*-This different thing has to do with a different woman.*

*-Come on Calypso… whatever it was, whoever she was, I don't*

*even recall it anymore.*

*-I got it. Do you still remember me at least?*

*-Always!*

*-Do you want me to be here when you return? -Ok, again the same old story... Do whatever you want! Only stop bothering me with your jealousy and hysteria. I have no time for such pettiness.*

*I had not time for cries and drama. I had to be ready for everything. I tried to locate my old friends because I sensed bad situations in the air. Harry was the only one who showed true interest in me. He called me every day and he promised me to come when it was time for me to give birth. Maurice seemed to have erased me from his memory and I believed that when the time arrived, I would be alone. I did not give many chances for Harry to keep his promise, but at least it was a relief that I would not be alone.*

*Maurice appeared suddenly one night in bad shape. Thin, drunk, unable to open the outer door. I helped him as much as I could, he lay on the sofa. He wanted me near him. He hugged me and cried.*

*-I am sorry my baby! I did not want to hurt you. Without you I can't live. If you are lost like Maya (his daughter) I will kill myself. I will not take it anymore. Don't abandon me, please, I don't know what has taken me lately. I thought that every-thing was fine. That I had everything under control. The only thing I want is to be happy together. Nothing else...*

*A stream of words, and stream kisses and embraces. He says all this with absolute sincerity and clarity. I like him a lot to be able to hold it back on him. I kiss him, I press my cheek on his tears.*

*-Everything will be fine.*

*To believe in myself.*

*He slept exhausted on my lap. Shortly I tugged him on the sofa, and I stood across from him. I was observing him. All night long! Not by fear for something to happen to him! I was looking at him trying to calm down my anger. How could he love me, as he pretended, and at the same time hurt me like this? Why things couldn't be simpler? I hated myself, the baby inside me that was ready to be born, him. I curded Michalis who had abandoned me, Orestes who dies, Theseus who was a piece of shit and I felt that I could even kill the guy who was sleeping opposite me, simply because he was a man. He could pay himself for every previous man. For all men! I stood above his head, and I felt death approaching that it was unbearable. I could cut his skull into two pieces with just one movement.*

*The next morning, when he came to his senses, I announced to him that after the birth of our child, I would leave the house.*

*-No, Calypso. I am not ready to exit this relationship. Neither did you. I know that you still love me. What you don't know though is how much I love you!*

*I look at him. Every part of my body wants to believe him, but my mind reacts.*

*-I made mistakes. Many! I know I hurt you. I know how important it is for you to have a steady and peaceful love relationship. I had promised you that I will always be here for you. That everything will go well!*

*He bends and pleads on my knees while hiding his face in my hands.*

*-My world has been shattered from one moment to the other. I lost control. I realized how little and unimportant I am. I have no words. Only don't leave! I have a lot of love for you inside me. If you give me a chance, I can amend everything.*

*She also bends in front of him.*

*-If you hurt me again like this, I will kill you with my own hands, she says and means every single word.*

*-Never again! We will be again as before. I, you, and our little miracle. My heart will beat only for you two. My life, your life!*

*-I still love you so much! I must be completely crazy and stupid at the same time; I tell myself with a sad smile.*

*-Me too! He tells her and he kisses her in his own unique way that takes her breath away each time.*

*-How about throwing a wedding party?*

*It was not exactly the marriage proposal I had imagined, but life until then had not gone exactly as I had imagined it either.*

*Finally, I was not alone the day I gave birth to our child. Harry arrived the last moment, Dido showed up from nowhere, because she happened to be in New York for a series of shows, I talked with my mother and my sister after almost ten years of silence and Maurice was next to me without break, an example of love and devotion. I learned from my old friends, Yorgos and Eleni that Alexandra had been released from jail and lived in Metsovo and that Andreas had opened a business in Bali with his German partner. The group that had been the cause for my acquaintance with Maurice threw a party for the arrival of our baby in a club and there we gathered all of us a few days after my exit from the hospital.*

*I thought that I had finally come to a happy ending! Naively thinking I always believed in fairy tales. In August I was dressed as a bride and before Christmas I became a widow.*

*I only was away one day. We worked together ten full years and I remember that I only missed a day. I was waiting for him at his office to do the last corrections. We were putting the last touches in his latest book. We had a relationship so powerful and particular. Beyond respect, love, and admiration. I loved him and I admired him. But most of all, he was the man who made me want to become better. To give the best out of me.*

*He was the only one who had told me:*

*-"Go ahead! I believe in you. Everything will be fine. Only never give up."*

*Truth or lie, it helped me. I believed in myself, and I regained my lost self-confidence. And we found him that day with a rope on his neck. He did not seem that he would depart like this. It did not suit him.*

*- "No, I had not understood anything! We lived together, yes... but I was not with him that morning. I left earlier. I had to take the baby to the doctor... it had fever. I am sorry!"*

*I still can't take away the thought that perhaps it would have been up to me to avoid this end. That I should have foreseen what has happened. For many years this thought kept torturing me! I am still trying to remember if the previous night had done or said something that would give me a hint that something was wrong, that somehow, he had asked for my help, and I missed it.*

*Sometimes he still comes at night, his remembrance relaxing in my eyes like a veil of tears. Maurice had done so many things for me and I, the only perhaps time that he needed my help, I was not next to him. And I was supposed to know everything about him. About his failed marriages, the minor who in her attempt to seduce him she had made a suicide attempt, his only daughter whom he adored but whom her mother – his youth fault—had taken her away from him. About his books, his bright career, his travels, his knowledge about things that few know, his love for cold pizza in the morning, his soft spot for expensive restaurants and fine wine... So many little and big things! As many as they can fit in ten full, lively, and joyful years. I ought to have understood it so many years together. Yes, he was a friendly, dynamic, and creative type. Only something in his slightly cross-eyed gaze seemed different. There was something more intense than it should have been.*

*Maurice committed suicide. The official report was maniac depression. When I entered the car the next day to go to his funeral, I wore his sunglasses. They still had his skin oil on them. I did not wipe it off. I was trying in any possible way to keep him alive.*

*I remember a month before Maurice's death, we met by chance Michalis in New York in a night club. When back then everything seemed to be fine. We did not exchange any word, only a few glances and a photograph. Summer, on the island, and two sunburnt faces that gaze uneasy and smiling at the camera. It was the sole souvenir of a love that died out early. Death however has nothing to do with life and it was time now to let remembrance aside and take its appropriate place. I left the picture on the table, and I left with Maurice.*

# EPILOGUE

*She returned to Greece almost twenty years later. She went with her children and Theo to her favorite beach. The same beach where she had escaped so many times when stress cut her breath away. She attempted to re-experience the calmness of her childhood, when all her life was ahead of her and hoped that she would achieve a great accomplishment. A time when all her world was small and simple. When feelings were intense and unique. Yet to no avail. Her mind was elsewhere. Perhaps her eyes had seen a lot by now.*

*Her kids were diving from her favorite rock. She was observing them to go up and down in its harsh edge and she felt intensely her mother's presence next to her. Like this her heart was beating for her many years ago, when life was simple, and her only fear was not to crush due to her audacious games; when her mother was looking at her growing up and designed a life for her daughter who nevertheless refused to accept.*

*No matter how hard she tried, she did not find the calm of her childhood. It was so naïve on her behalf to believe that a particular place has the power to appease the turmoil of so many years and places. She found though another kind of peace. Equally warm and sweet. She found the peacefulness of the blessed moment that one knows, as time goes by, that perhaps they might never come back again. She found the invaluable peace of mind that no one can take away from you simply because you carry it within yourself, like your heart.*

*"I don't chase time anymore. We are friends now. We move in parallel orbits without obvious competition. I know that time will win in the end. Like death. This is why I am not afraid. I*

*gazed at him upfront several times up to this moment. It shuttered my soul each time he took away from me beloved people. It pushed me deep down with Orestes, my grandmother, Maurice. With the couple of the opposite house, with the friend who departed from this world, with Greece who has been lost. I think however that I did not fear death when I touched his lips.*

*My life was fulfilled. Full of mistakes, passions, friends, joy, sadness, images. I changed. Within me Vassiliki and Calypso continue struggling about who will domineer, but Vassiliki has learned by now how to manage the immature, tragic calypso. Despite my new attitude toward life, naively thinking, I keep believing in fairy tales. The evenings when my family sets quiet, I unlock the cubicle of little Calypso and I follow her to walk like a fairy in the paths of her world. She does not run any more like a beast chased by qualms and ghosts. The Furies disappeared a long time ago. Now she wanders alone in the world of the other looking for company. Just before dawn's coming, she returns exhausted to her glass world and I myself to my own world. No one knows about these secret meetings of ours.*

*After the many tough lessons, I came to the conclusion that the only feet that are able to support you in life are your own. Loves, flowers, glass worlds and multi-colored feathers are able only to disorient you. These are only able to weaken you and make you throw your arms and weapons. Never, not even for a moment it is worthy to exchange your invaluable freedom with the false security of a permanent relationship. For nothing is permanent, not even your own life.*

*In the final word, I have been lucky. Orestes' death which deprived me of a life as I had imagined it in a peaceful country, saved me! I left with my head bent from a country that still respected itself. I left when Greece was still proud. I lived another life in an adopted country, and I always was different from its other children. I looked foreign and my mentality was different. I always felt like an adopted child whose mother gave it in the hope of retrieving it back one day in the future, but things exacerbated, and she never returned to get it back. And the child wasted her life with her eyes fixed on the street, waiting for the warm hug of the mother.*

*I learned and I suffered. I fell down many times and I was forced to gather my pieces again and again. I kept believing in myself when few still supported me. And I continued pushing invisible walls and building glass bridges. I grabbed myself from the dream because it was the only thing that could keep me alive. And when sometimes I succeeded and I took a breath, my world had nothing to do with the world of my imagination. Yet it was my own!*

*I don't daydream anymore. I live the day as it comes, and I feel grateful for everything good that happens around me. I learned to be grateful for things that in the past I considered a given. Things like my health, my beloved's health, the food on our table, the coziness of our home, Theo's love, the smile of the unknown pedestrian to whom I give priority, the cleanliness of the air that I inhale, my good neighbors who contribute to the order, music, my routine.*

*I keep longing for the perfumes, colors, music, my country's people, and I continue to believe that one day I will return. The more time passes by the more hope dies out. The lightest sleep*

*I continue to have it in my childhood room, but it does not exist anymore, as the country that I loved does not exist anymore either. There is only a sweet remembrance, many justifications and in between them many fragile glass bridges".*

www.ingramcontent.com/pod-product-compliance
Lightning Source LLC
Chambersburg PA
CBHW051526120626
46551CB00012B/1104